THE SIMPLE
WORDSWORTH

THE SIMPLE WORDSWORTH

Studies
in the Poems
1797 - 1807

by

JOHN F. DANBY

Routledge & Kegan Paul

LONDON

First published 1960
by Routledge & Kegan Paul Ltd
Broadway House, Carter Lane
London EC4V 5EL

Reprinted 1968, 1971

Printed by offset in Great Britain
by Alden & Mowbray Ltd
at the Alden Press, Oxford

ISBN 0 7100 1252 7

TO BEN POMERANCE

Rare poems ask rare friends

BEN JONSON

CONTENTS

ACKNOWLEDGEMENTS

Parts of the first three chapters of this book have appeared in *The Cambridge Journal*—now, unfortunately, no longer in existence. I would like to thank the former editors for permission to use again the material they were good enough to print. I should also like to thank my colleagues for their comment, and for their collateral work: Mr. A. E. Dyson and Mr. W. J. B. Owen whose interests have taken them into related fields, and Mr. R. W. King for his early reading and comment. I ought, too, to thank my students for their reactions, whichever way, but always instructive, to the matter that follows; and my daughters Jane and Helena for invaluable help with proofs.

The references are to the E. de Selincourt edition of the poems, except that for *Lyrical Ballads* itself I have used the edition of T. Hutchinson. The quotations from *The Prelude* are from the version of 1805.

J.F.D.

PROLOGUE

IN spite of Wordsworth's place in the canon one cannot be sure that he is nowadays read. Wordsworth has tended to be swallowed up in a general 'Wordsworthianism' or in the anti-Wordsworthianism of those who have reacted against it. Certainly only a minority, it would seem, read him with the exciting shock of surprise and delight that is central to the experience good poetry offers—or with the close attention good poetry deserves. The idol of Wordsworth's friends has been the aunt-sally of his foes. Yet one feels Wordsworth himself still remains aloof, untouched by the better part of the discussion. What he rated high his best supporters have tended to rate low. The poems he especially prized his readers have smiled at as forgivable aberrations: 'Simon Lee', 'The Thorn', 'The Reverie of Poor Susan'—in the main, most of those poems put into *Lyrical Ballads* as *exempla* of a new mode of sensibility and a new non-septic manner of writing.

The partisans of Wordsworth were slow in coming forward. When they did appear they seemed already destined to be Victorians—a generation too early weaned, premature adults fulfilling wishfully the dislocated desires of adolescence in a backward-looking middle-age, finding in Wordsworth a consolation and support he might himself have had grave doubts about: doubts as to whether it should be supplied, or was in fact supplied, by the universe he himself had experienced. John Stuart Mill's is a *locus classicus* of commendation:

> In the first place, these poems addressed themselves powerfully to one of the strongest of my pleasurable susceptibilities, the love of rural objects and natural scenery; to which I had been indebted not only for much of the pleasure of my life, but quite recently for one of my longest relapses into depression. In this power of rural beauty over me there was a foundation laid for taking pleasure in Wordsworth's poetry; the more so, as his scenery lies mostly among mountains, which, owing to my early Pyrenean excursion, were my ideal of natural beauty. But Wordsworth would never have had any great effect on me, if he had merely placed before me beautiful pictures of natural scenery. Scott does this still better than Wordsworth, and a very second-rate landscape does it more effectually than any poet. What made Wordsworth's poems a medicine for my state of mind, was that they expressed, not mere outward beauty, but states of feeling, and of thought coloured by feeling, under the excitement of beauty. They seemed to be the very culture of the feelings, which I was in quest of. In them I seemed to draw from a source of inward joy, of sympathetic and imaginative pleasure, which could be shared in by all human beings; which had no connexion with struggle or imperfection, but would be made richer by every improvement in the physical or social condition of man kind. From them I seemed to learn what would be the perennial sources of happiness, when all the greater evils of life shall have been removed.
>
> (*Autobiography*, p. 125. Oxford Classics, 1924)

But one wonders if 'Oenone' or 'The Lotus Eaters' had been available would Mill's testimonial have been made out to Wordsworth? A taste for 'rural beauty' does not seem a safe or necessary qualification for reading his poems. And in this respect, Mill judged, even Scott was the better purveyor. 'States of feeling, and of thought coloured by feeling, under the excitement of beauty'—this is an odd way of describing Wordsworth's best achievements as a poet. But, as Mill again reassures us (and here he must have had Tennyson, or Browning, or Patmore, or Meredith in mind?)

2

'There have certainly been, even in our own age, greater poets than Wordsworth'. So, it would seem, Wordsworth's place in Mill's biography is only accidental: almost any other good poet could have proved that even after utopia was realized there would still be something to live for, something for the liberal to read.

Matthew Arnold was introduced to Wordsworth by way of Dr. Arnold and the rigours of holidays in the Lakes. When he writes that Wordsworth 'laid us on the flowery lap of earth' we are entitled to be doubly sceptical. Surely it was no flowery lap that Dr. Arnold would suggest to the over-strained doubter. Furthermore, the phrase seems to reverse the whole tenor of Wordsworth's meaning. The 'aching pleasures' of nature, in Wordsworth's development, were replaced by a 'still sad music of humanity'. Similarly, Wordsworth's flower will come ultimately to be the celandine, stiff, and open to the battering hail. Arnold's 'flowery lap' is as inappropriate to the Wordsworthian as Mill's 'rural beauty'.

And so on. Wordsworth became part of the Wordsworthianism that has blanketed his poems and prevented them from being read, part of an urban cult of 'nature', or a chief witness against the spirit of Victorian doubt to a benevolent universe and man's place in it as favourite son. Aldous Huxley's 'Wordsworth in the Tropics' is a smart rejoinder: Wordsworth's view would not last a moment if the jungle as well as the Cumberland Moors were thought of as 'natural'.

The most important voice in the twentieth century to be raised on Wordsworth's side was that of A. N. Whitehead. Whitehead's nature is not that of the Wordsworthian. He claims, however, it is similar to the nature Wordsworth himself responded to:

> the romantic reaction started neither with God nor with Lord Bolingbroke, but with nature. We are here witnessing a conscious reaction against the whole tone of the eighteenth century. That

3

century approached nature with the abstract analysis of science, whereas Wordsworth opposes to the scientific abstractions his full concrete experience. . . . He always grasps the whole of nature as involved in the tonality of the particular instance. . . . Wordsworth, to the height of genius, expresses the concrete facts of our apprehension, facts which are distorted in the scientific analysis.

(Science and the Modern World)

Whitehead, the philosopher, does not talk about Wordsworth's philosophy. What he has in mind is something that can only be apprehended by responding fully to Wordsworth's poetry. Any philosophy we might abstract from that poetry would be merely, in Whitehead's view, another distortion.

Whitehead's perception has characteristic breadth and depth. He is a useful counterpoise to Mill, and to all those who would *make use* of Wordsworth: either to find consolation, or to illustrate a 'movement' in literature, or to exemplify a psychological thesis: the effects of thwarted love (Annette Vallon) or of suppressed incestuousness (Dorothy). More important still, Whitehead writes of Wordsworth as if his work were of contemporary, perennially contemporary, importance. He avoids assimilating him to eighteenth-century origins in Hartley, Adam Smith, Priestley, Akenside, Thomson, or Young.

Wordsworth can be seen maybe more clearly now than at any time since his death. In a more special sense than that which applies to all good poets he is our contemporary. His age, like ours, was one in which frontiers were moving. When he was born the Elder Pitt was still alive; Disraeli and Gladstone were already established politicians when he died. To the period of his life (to his friend Coleridge as well as to Kierkegaard) have been traced the beginnings of Existentialism. The moving frontiers were many and various. All of them, then as now, intersected inside the individual, dividing him every way. If we can still use the word 'modern' to cover a period that might already be past, Wordsworth

4

writes at the beginning of the modern age—an age called upon to ask itself, anxiously and self-consciously, 'Who is the Happy Warrior?' Wordsworth had heard the call. He had also undergone experiences which bore in upon him that he was especially endowed to find the answers. In *The Prelude* he tells of the important moments:

> As on I walked, a comfort seem'd to touch
> A heart that had not been disconsolate,
> Strength came where weakness was not known to be,
> At least not felt; and restoration came,
> Like an intruder, knocking at the door
> Of unacknowledg'd weariness. I took
> The balance in my hand and weigh'd myself.
>
> *(Prelude* IV, ll. 143–9)

Or, this time returning from a dance, in the same first long vacation from Cambridge:

> to the brim
> My heart was full; I made no vows, but vows
> Were then made for me; bond unknown to me
> Was given, that I should be, else sinning greatly,
> A dedicated spirit.
>
> *(Prelude* IV, ll. 341–344)

The experience guaranteed its own truth. Though it came to him it was not of him. The weakness replaced by strength was not even realized to be such until it was removed. The vows made were not personal resolutions. The paradoxes make us gasp that they are not already commonplaces.

It was this, of course, that made Wordsworth uniquely confident for a 'modern'. It was for this strength of confidence the stricken natures of the nineteenth century after him would turn back to his poetry. Equally, it is the immediacy of the experiential certainty which separates Wordsworth from his eighteenth-century precursors. Wordsworth's vows were not personal wishes, nor was his faith a deduction: both were grounded in a *datum* of experience. The tone of the

Prefaces and of the *Advertisement to Lyrical Ballads* is decided by this. It is the tone of the prophet or seer, the tone of the Old Testament.

But while there is this private basis for the Wordsworthian achievement, and while there is truth in the claim for his 'perennial contemporaneity', it must not be forgotten that Wordsworth was not alone in his insights, and that he was very much a man of his time. The literary revolution he is identified with was part of a wider series of non-literary changes. However unique his reaction is in some ways, Wordsworth shares common ground with his major contemporaries, with Coleridge and Blake certainly.

All three saw their break with a literary manner as being also a break with what the whole era of 1660–1760 implied. For Blake one of the reigning demons of this period was Newton, identified sometimes with Urizen or, at other times, with Satan. Newton is not exactly a Wordsworthian *bête noire*. However, the line describing him in the 1805 version of *The Prelude* ('Newton with his Prism and silent Face') is much less sympathetic than that substituted for it in the version of 1850: 'Voyaging through strange seas of Thought, alone.' Wordsworth and Coleridge did not express the matter mythopoeically as Blake did. They had, however, some of the same things in mind. Both would agree with Blake that the preceding age was the age of Urizen, that it was an irrational world (as Whitehead too might put it) of *imposed* 'rational' law. Coleridge's account in *The Friend* is compendious enough:

> mechanical philosophy . . . a system of natural rights instead of social and hereditary privileges—acquiescence in historical testimony substituted for faith, and yet the true historical feeling . . openly stormed or perilously undermined. . . . Imagination excluded from Poesy, and fancy paramount in physics; the eclipse of the ideal by the mere shadow of the sensible.

> (*The Friend*, Bohn. Edn. pp. 296–7)

The Newtonian universe is familiar to us now (and we

might still be inclined to summarize it so) in terms of its limitations. It opened out awesomely into Pascal's two infinities, it then proceeded to measure and domesticate these by the newly invented calculus. Everything in this universe was explicable except existence itself. Voltaire, therefore, was serious when he joked that if God did not exist he would have to be invented. Again, the God needed to maintain the cosmic clock need only be a clock-maker, and an absentee. Regarded in its total perfection the universe bore witness to a Supreme Architect, and He could be deduced from and then identified with the marvellous whole. All the same, as Auden has pointed out, God could not enter into His creation in any of its parts. Incarnation was inconceivable. Literally, as Blake perceived, Voltaire's God was Nobody's Daddy. And along with incarnation, the possibility of those instants of revelation and participation which Wordsworth experienced was also excluded:

> There is a field, of many, one,
> A single tree that I have looked upon.

—Wordsworth's tree, for the eighteenth century, would be as unthinkable as the burning bush. Change, growth, emergence of the unique—all were reduced to aggregation, rearrangement, alteration of position. Space and time in this universe were *continua* of basically uniform points: though Blake would assert there was one moment of each day Satan-Newton could not catch, and that that moment opened into Eternity.

Plain man, philosopher, crank, and mystic objected as the century wore on, with equal right, to the abstraction imposed. The romantic reaction is a reaction of all four, together or in varying combinations. The plain man knew at first hand that harmony was not the main character of his human condition, and could scarcely be a fair deduction from experience. The philosopher would come to see that poetry and push-pin are not the same, nor 'ought' and 'is'.

7

At any time the crank is a misfit demanding his own special explanation. The mystic was quite prepared to live without those ideas he could neither live with nor live towards.

For the plain man (so much the great romantics' central concern) harmony was the absentee, and God the possible presence. Society during the pre-romantic period did not amount to a system of pre-established mutual benefactions, neither to the disfranchised Yorkshire manufacturers nor to the London Working Men's Corresponding Societies. Methodism took root among both. Its voice was heard by Peter Bell and helped to frighten him into softness of heart. It sang of the end of the Newtonian 'systems' in a final conflagration:

> Then let the thundering trumpet sound,
>   The latest lightning glare,
> The mountains melt, the solid ground
>   Dissolve as liquid air;
>
> The huge celestial bodies roll,
>   Amidst that general fire,
> And shrivel as a parchment scroll,
>   And all in smoke expire. . . .
>
> So be it, let this system end,
>   This ruinous earth and skies,
> The new Jerusalem descend,
>   The new creation rise.
>
> (Wesley's *Hymns*, 1876, No. 64)

But Methodism was more than a mere outlet for apocalyptic hope. Charles Wesley addressed a God neither absentee nor comfortable to know:

> Deepen the wound Thy hands have made
>   In this weak, helpless soul,
> Till mercy, with its balmy aid,
>   Descends to make me whole.

8

The sharpness of thy two-edged sword
    Enable me to endure;
Till bold to say, My hallowing Lord
    Hath wrought a perfect cure.

(*Hymns*, No. 370)

However much it could be thought to be so, the world of
the eighteenth century could not actually be felt to be the
best of all possible. Nor could the middle-class reformer (the
liberal conscience of the eighteenth century) finally reduce
his best motives to self-interest or to pleasure. The problem
ultimately for men of good will (as Coleridge early discovered in *Religious Musings*) was the problem of the martyr:
willing the sword with which those wound him for whom—
and for whose greater happiness—he dies. Sympathy with
suffering might have its own obscure self-congratulation, but
not suffering on behalf of those who were scarcely aware they
were in pain. And the romantic revolution was originally the
revolt of a middle class ready for martyrdom, self-avowed
men of good will.

All this is fairly commonplace but needs briefly pointing
to before the 'literary' revolution of Blake, Wordsworth and
Coleridge can be approached. Literary revolutions, notori-
ously, are only aspects of changes affecting a wider field. The
romantic need for a new mode of writing reflected the need
for a new world, for the marriage, Blake would call it, of
both the worlds:

The new Jerusalem descend,
The new creation rise.

The break-up of the Newtonian universe signals disturb-
ances in every sphere of human activity: the intellectual,
religious, ethical, political, and social. Politically, the Whig
Oligarchy was disintegrating. Middle-class moralist pres-
sure-groups were replacing country-house managers. (Wordsworth refused the living which John Robinson, the great
arranger of Whig patronage, could have procured for him as

a needy relative.) The two-party system of the nineteenth century was struggling into existence. In philosophy the age of Locke and Hartley was yielding to something Kantian and Germanic; in science, instead of the dominance of physics and mechanics (the world of Newton) there was the excitement of chemistry and electricity (the new world of Priestley and Davy); in religion, instead of deism a new theology, dialectical and trinitarian, with the beginnings of which Coleridge is immediately associated. The period is one, as we have said, of moving frontiers. For the middle-class well-wisher caught by compassion in a lower-class ferment, or for the partisan of humanity-in-general who found the revolutionary struggle issuing into a clash of national loyalties, the frontiers, then as now, passed through and divided the individual. The period 1760–1830 sees the beginnings of 'Angst'.

Listed like this the changes in the Wordsworthian period seem formidable and might sound pretentious. And what, it might be asked, is the relevance of such a list to understanding the simple Wordsworth who wrote 'A Rainbow'?

There is a right instinct behind such scepticism. It has been only too easy to turn away from Wordsworth's poems to his 'theories', his 'philosophy'. To illustrate at the same time his revolutionary position in literature and philosophy, let us compare Wordsworth's 'A Rainbow' with some lines written on the rainbow in 1727.

In that year Sir Isaac Newton died and James Thomson wrote at length in blank verse to honour the occasion:

> Th' aerial flow of Sound was known to him,
> From whence it first in wavy circles breaks,
> Till the touch'd organ takes the message in.
> Nor could the darting beam of speed immense,
> Escape his swift pursuit, and measuring eye.
> Even Light itself, which everything displays,
> Shone undiscover'd till his brighter mind
> Untwisted all the shining robe of day;

And, from the whitening undistinguish'd blaze,
Collecting every ray into his kind,
To the charm'd eye educ'd the gorgeous train
Of Parent-colours. First the flaming Red
Sprung vivid forth; the tawny Orange next;
And next delicious Yellow; by whose side
Fell the kind beams of all-refreshing Green.
Then the pure Blue, that swells autumnal skies,
Etherial play'd; and then, of sadder hue,
Emerg'd the deepened Indigo, as when
The heavy-skirted evening droops with frost.
While the last gleamings of refracted light
Dy'd in the fainting Violet away.
These, when the clouds distil the rosy shower,
Shine out distinct adown the watery bow;
While o'er our heads the dewy vision bends
Delightful, melting on the fields beneath.
Myriads of mingling dyes from these result,
And myriads still remain; infinite source
Of beauty, ever blushing, ever new!
Did ever poet image aught so fair,
Dreaming in whispering groves, by the hoarse brook!
Or prophet, to whose rapture Heaven descends!
Even now the setting sun and shifting clouds,
Seen, Greenwich, from thy lovely heights, declare
How just, how beauteous, the 'refractive' law.

Thomson's lines are enormously assured and confident:

Untwisted *all* the shining robe of day.

That is better than Keats's line about philosophy (i.e.
science) unweaving the rainbow. It is also, incidentally, a
richer and more accurate metaphor. The force is in 'all'.
Thomson really means it. Newton's achievement is inclusive
and final. *All* the universe is at last known completely: for all
men, and for always. Poetry now will have this certain and
absolute truth to base itself upon. In a sense poetry will be
secondary. It will exist to expound, to apply, to decorate or

persuasively recommend those truths not poets but scientists
have laid bare:

> Did ever poet image aught so fair,
> Dreaming in whispering groves, by the hoarse brook!
> Or prophet, to whose rapture Heaven descends!

Thomson is glad that everything—including poetry—can
now settle down: the essential work is finished.

Thomson wrote in the golden age of the Newtonian assurance: in the age of Physics. Wordsworth writes, if we might
indulge the fancy, in the age of Chemistry. The difference
between the two sciences in Wordsworth's time was exciting,
more apparent then than later in the nineteenth century. In
physics one worked with mathematics and measurement.
Chemists, of course, in the long run, were to do so too. But
in the late eighteenth century the chemist is someone capable
of being portrayed, as Dalton was, kneeling beside a bog
collecting marsh gas, helped by a small boy and his tiddlers'-
jar. In chemistry two different things are brought together, a
sudden interaction takes place, and instead of the two things
there is a third completely different from either. The universe of Newton was a complete, settled thing. Man's relation to it was either that of spectator or of fixed part in a
stable whole. The universe of chemistry is a universe of
action and re-action, of formation and transformation. Man
in this universe is not a spectator. He is an identity both
acting and re-acting, formed and formative.

It may be fanciful to describe Wordsworth's as the poetry
of chemistry, romantically understood. He did himself, however, use the language of action and re-action to define the
experience put into his poetry. And the chemical analogy is
useful to suggest the difference between Thomson's world
and his, between the lines 'To the Memory of Sir Isaac
Newton' and 'A Rainbow':

> My heart leaps up when I behold
> A rainbow in the sky:

So was it when my life began;
  So is it now I am a man;
So be it when I shall grow old,
  Or let me die!
The Child is father of the Man,
  And I would wish my days to be
Bound each to each by natural piety.

In Wordsworth's poem there is the rainbow and the man
and the re-action that takes place when the two come
together. Wordsworth is not arranging products that have
been passed on to him from some other centre of truth-
making for tastefully decorative treatment. The emphasis is
on action between, on what it would be maybe fashionable
to call 'dialogue'. Things can and do happen in the universe.
The universe involves process, formation, and transformation. Because of this Wordsworth starts with the 'now' of
particular experience. Then, since persons are themselves
growing things involved in the process of a unified life, he
recalls his first childhood's reaction and immediately after
looks forward to old age. Then, he hopes, the capacity to
respond, or at least to remember, will still be with him.
Or else let him die: for will he not be already dead?—We
hardly ever read the poem with full understanding because
of its over-quoted and over-misunderstood lines:

The Child is father of the Man:
And I would wish my days to be
Bound each to each by natural piety.

'Natural piety' has nothing to do with 'nature' in the hikers'
sense. And the piety is not church-bound. Wordsworth is
thinking, as the psychiatrists do, of how one lived experience
interacts with all the others, and how the unified and harmonious mind is ideally one in which youth, maturity, and
age continue to reflect and regenerate each other. The Child
is father of the Man. The parent principle of continuing
growth *is* the power of fresh response. On this man depends

still for all those moments of renewable experience he is capable of. While this remains with him his days can be bound each to each, in that relation of mutual trust and respect which constitutes 'pietas'.

We began by doubting if Wordsworth today is *read*. The chapters that follow will attempt a reading of the younger Wordsworth. The years 1797–1807 are generally agreed to cover the best of his work, the problematic Wordsworth of *Lyrical Ballads* as well as the Wordsworth who expounded and explained himself in the early version of *The Prelude*. *The Prelude* itself is not included in this essay: my excuse is that Wordsworth did not choose to publish it in his lifetime. The main concern will be with the 'simple' Wordsworth who underwent the interesting spiritual journey from 'The Reverie of Poor Susan' to 'The White Doe of Rylstone', two poems, one at either end of his most positively creative period, which have been, I think, unnecessarily misconceived—unnecessarily and harmfully.

I

WORDSWORTH AND
SIMPLICITY

I

THERE is a plausible theory that a poem is—and is only
—the words on the page, and that to discuss therefore the
writer's intentions is fallacious: we cannot know what he had
in his mind. Part of the paralysing fright in the suggestion
comes from its reinforcement by our awareness of the existence of mechanical brains, and the logical possibility that in
an indefinitely long time a monkey on a typewriter would
jumble out a Shakespeare play. The fallacy of the 'fallacy of
intention' is that the author's meaning for a reader includes
his intentions. The nightmare of the mechanical poem-
maker can be dispelled by considering that in no possible
time could another machine be devised to read what the first
had 'written'. Words exist not on the page but between
people: only people can *mean* anything.

Wordsworth certainly described himself as 'a man talking
to men'. He felt, furthermore, in doing so, a special responsibility. Poems alter persons. The poet can make and also
unmake. Evil communications corrupt good manners. And
it was against a corruption in literature and life that Wordsworth set himself. The moment of dedication recorded in

The Prelude laid on him a charge. The Preface to *Lyrical Ballads* (second edition) is militantly astringent:

> . . . habits of meditation have, I trust, so prompted and regulated my feelings, that my descriptions of such objects as strongly excite those feelings, will be found to carry along with them a *purpose*. If this opinion be erroneous, I can have little right to the name of a Poet.   (II. p. 387)

The poet has to be a certain sort of man before he has the right to address himself to men. Though, in poetry, a man must use words, it is the man not the words that signify. If the paradox might stand in regard to a literary innovator who made it his prime task to clear away certain literary vocabularies in favour of others, Wordsworth, at heart, we might say, was profoundly uninterested in poetry as words. For Wordsworth the converse of the proposition that poetry is words would be nearer the truth. For both him and Coleridge, poetry had to be proportionable, as they said, to the real or desirable sympathies of mankind. This meant that the poet must be expert in the real and the desirable, and aim his poems in accordance with the priorities decided upon. Far from imagining the poet as one chiefly endowed with 'the lovely gift of the gab', Wordsworth could even conceive of what he termed (itself a revolutionary shift in point of view) 'the silent poet'. His brother John (drowned at sea in 1805) was one such:

> Thou, a schoolboy, to the sea hadst carried
> Undying recollections: Nature there
> Was with thee; she, who loved us both, she still
> Was with thee; and even so didst thou become
> A *silent* Poet; from the solitude
> Of the vast sea didst bring a watchful heart
> Still couchant, an inevitable ear,
> And an eye practised like a blind man's touch.
>
> (II, p. 122)

Such too were the simple word-deprived countrymen he knew in Cumberland:

16

> Others, too,
> There are among the walks of homely life
> Still higher, men for contemplation framed,
> Shy, and unpractis'd in the strife of phrase,
> Meek men, whose very souls perhaps would sink
> Beneath them, summon'd to such intercourse;
> Theirs is the language of the heavens, the power,
> The thought, the image, and the silent joy;
> Words are but under-agents in their souls;
> When they are grasping in their greatest strength
> They do not breathe among them.
>
> (*Prelude* XII, ll. 264–74)

As against the poem-machine, then, Wordsworth would point out that the poet has a responsibility the machine has not. He must decide between human priorities. The poet is a man first, with real—and maybe as he hopes—desirable sympathies. As against the silent poets, it is his task to use words. While he must draw on the same sources of wisdom and strength as they do he is committed as they are not to the public necessity of utterance: otherwise the sources of strength the silent poets resort to might either dry up or their location be lost.

Wordsworth is still in the great Renaissance tradition which saw in the poet a responsible human spokesman. As against the eighteenth century he must insist on a reconstitution of 'the truth'. His view of what is to be inculcated will be different from that of a poet like Thomson, but poetry, he will agree, must continue to be both moral and didactic. Moral edification, however, is not now with him a matter of verbal precept. Rather, it is the embodiment of living occasions in words, the admission of the reader through words into the remoulding experience. It is in fact poems: poems 'proper', as poems, after the romantics, will be considered to be. A new standard of actuality in poetry is insisted upon, a new conception of what poets should be, a new understanding of how their words actually work upon their audience.

The poet is responsible in a new way to his world, to himself, and to his readers.

'Under-agents of the soul'—once words are seen in this light a fresh approach can be made both to the Wordsworthian revolution and to the general problem of simplicity in poetry which it forces forward. Simplicity is Wordsworth's main concern. How, in poems, does 'simplicity' work?

At maybe the most primitive level words are under-agents often to pre-verbal things. They can be merely phatic expressions indicating pain, joy, sadness, *etc.*, and unless we recognize the situations which literally ex-press the noises the expressions so-called will be meaningless. Some good poetry (Schiller might say it was the voice of 'nature') comes near to a simplicity of this sort:

> Westron wind, when wilt thou blow,
> The small rain down might rain?
> Christ, that my love were in my arms
> And I in my bed again!

or Wordsworth's (though it is rare for him to write in this way):

> But she is in her grave, and, oh,
> The difference to me!

It is little good denying poetry of this kind its place or its occasional power. Language in these cases, as with the emotional scream, is the under-agent of situation. The words call out from an implied dramatic setting. The situation implied—and our response to what it means—the words as such have little control over. We are as unaware of them as we should be of the glass in a window. Wordsworth's 'A Rainbow' is dramatic in this sense, though already more elaborately so. It is a poem in so far as we appreciate the rich setting, the whole suppressed drama of Wordsworth's new stance, his novel address to the universe.

A related case of 'simplicity' as expression of feeling from

a given situation is exemplified in poems like Tennyson's
'The Charge of the Light Brigade':

> Half a league, half a league,
> Half a league onward,
> All in the valley of Death
> Rode the six hundred.

There are feelings fitting into real situations (like this one of
Tennyson's, where many men were going needlessly to
death and glory) which might be called primal. Not to
respond to such a situation as the poem celebrates, and
respond even in what Richards would call a 'stock' way,
would be to fall short of common humanity. The old lady
who cries at the thought of all the mothers' sons going off to
war is not to be despised. And the kind of poetry which taps
such primal feelings (Tennyson was a past-master of it) is
not on that account despicable. Feelings of this kind are
what Auden has called, in connexion with Tennyson, the
nursery feelings: meaning by that not that they are weak
and childish but rather that they are overpowering and
human. With such feelings it would be truer to say that the
feeling has us rather than that we have it: the feeling pos-
sesses us as hunger, fear, love, or despair can possess the
child.

It might be that maturity consists in our ability to win
power over such feelings—so that instead of them possessing
us we possess them. But precisely what this means it would
be hard to say. Fully to contain the feeling inside one is
maybe to have the feeling and to retain the capacity to admit
at least the possibility of other feelings at the same time, to
see other aspects of the situation, even to see the feeling
itself in perspective. (In the *Valediction of Weeping*, for example, Donne feels as powerfully as Tennyson could, but
he feels with more of himself. Parts of himself are weighing
the feeling, considering, assessing, judging it.) Maybe it is
true that the poetry of feeling which swamps the mind is

pernicious. Possibly Plato was right—if he were thinking only of such poetry—to banish it from the Republic. Certainly Wordsworth would approve of such a banishment. The metaphor of 'recollecting' emotion in tranquillity is essentially one of containment.

Where more than one feeling is entertained or considered admissible we are verging on a poetry that might seem the opposite of simple—the poetry of confusion, or conflict, or irony; poetry of the pun, of inconclusive syntax, of paradox, avowed ambiguity, and so on. Recent trends in criticism have led to a predominant concern with poetry of this type. Mr. Cleanth Brooks, indeed, has gone so far as to claim it as the highest type of poetry, and thus the highest manifestation of mind. Only irony, conflict, paradox can be the basis of poetry proper. Poems embrace the contraries life cannot reduce (without loss of content) to unity. Clearly this is not a view that the traditional poets have held, and certainly not Wordsworth.

Wordsworth's ideal was a kind of poetry that would include what Cleanth Brooks desiderates, but go beyond the point of complexity-as-hesitation and issue into the simplicity of integration. Poetry for Wordsworth is the utterance, ideally, of a responsive sensibility and a securely grounded judgement, acting together. Spontaneity in itself can be the rash-like irruption of trivialities. The poet's claim to attention is his practical acquaintance with what for men is important or unimportant. Ultimately the poet will be capable, owing to the discipline of habit, of only a special kind of spontaneity: most especially, of 'those thoughts and feelings which, by his own choice, or from the structure of his own mind, arise in him without immediate external excitement.'

Wordsworth is describing a process of disciplined self-integration which his best poetry, in fact, exemplifies. There is a poetry of simplicity, however, different from this, and different altogether from the other kinds already indicated. In this 'simplicity' all the effects ascribable to the arduous training of thought, feeling, and choice seem to be effortlessly brought off as if by an angelic intelligence, a 'schöne Seele', careless and undeliberating and unerringly right. Before returning to examine further Wordsworth's own simplicity we might look at an example of this other in Blake. The comparison of Wordsworth and Blake is a useful one.

'Infant Joy' is the apex of Blake's mind. It is also his least communicative of verbal utterances:

> 'I have no name:
> I am but two days old'—
> > What shall I call thee?
> 'I happy am,
> Joy is my name'.—
> > Sweet joy befall thee!
>
> Pretty Joy!
> Sweet Joy, but two days old.
> > Sweet Joy I call thee.
> Thou dost smile,
> I sing the while,
> > Sweet joy befall thee!

Verbal analysis here would not get us as far as the poem takes us. The poem is about . . . what exactly? The namelessness of newness and 'that'-ness, which even to categorize would be to reduce and distort, if indeed any category were applicable? The assertion, too, of the Joy that 'is' and 'is now' and 'is going to be'—the literally idiotic happiness of 'yes!' along with a glad grateful acceptance of its having happened? And with this, too, the implied hope, wish, and doubt of

> Sweet joy befall thee!

—Nothing of this could be proved. It would even be possible to dismiss the poem as silly. Yet . . .

> 'I have no name:
> I am but two days old'—

the situation is one that occurs every time a baby is born, and each time a uniqueness is smiled on, submitted to, accepted, and cherished. The union in the poem of tough, self-consisting joy, and awed, responding tenderness, of the dynamic and the vulnerable, is perfect.

'Infant Joy' brings out clearly another thing that needs to be borne in mind in the discussion of poems, especially 'simple' poems: that is the double relationship in which a poem stands, relations we might call intrinsic and extrinsic.

Intrinsic relations are those the words of the poem entertain between themselves. Every good poem has a natural cohesiveness; all its parts have dealings with each other and reinforce each other. The extrinsic relations are manifold. First there are such half-and-half verbal factors as pattern, structure, stanza, plotting, tone. The words have a shape and a voice—and these define themselves partly against the patterns and tones the writer is rejecting. What the poem 'is' (intrinsically) is maintained by and against what it 'is not'. A second extrinsic relation is that which a poem has in the setting of the poet's whole work. Poems talk to each other. With writers like Blake and Wordsworth we are dealing with poems as the utterances of persons. Here the vistas widen. They open out on the poet's knowledge of the viable means of communication, and (yet further) on to his command of what he has at his disposal to communicate—the 'matter' he can put into his poetry. The first of these is the poet's knowledge of words, in the widest interpretation of what this means, including, as Wordsworth was one of the first to point out, 'the various stages of meaning through which words have passed' (II, p. 389); also, the various decorums that have governed literary communications, and 'the multitude of causes' that combine socially to decide these. (The *Preface* of 1802 is one of the most remarkable documents we possess as proof of the profound and sophisticated insight a poet can have into the nature of his medium —meaning.) Even in the *Advertisement to Lyrical Ballads* of

1798 Wordsworth underlines the sense of responsibility and tradition which he and Coleridge shared: 'with few exceptions the Author believes that the language adopted in it [i.e. in 'The Rime of the Ancyent Marinere'] has been equally intelligible for these last three centuries'. In Wordsworth's own case, it will be remembered, in 1800–1 he was translating Chaucer, a few years later the sonnets of Michelangelo, and at all times saw himself in a line that went back through the seventeenth century and the great Renaissance to mediaeval forebears. That poets need to know 'words' in this widest sense Wordsworth insisted on in the *Advertisement*.

The poet's matter, i.e. what he has to say, is clearly extrinsic. This region he co-inhabits not only with 'mighty poets in their misery dead' but also with silent poets like Wordsworth's brother John and the Cumberland Statesmen. This sphere is clearly pre-verbal or post-verbal. It is what Wordsworth and the eighteenth century generally recognized as the sphere of Judgement: the human capacity to experience and to decide priorities among experiences, 'what is really important to men'. Judgement Wordsworth rated first in the hierarchy of endowments requisite for the poet:

> Judgment to decide how and where, and in what degree each of these [aforementioned] faculties ought to be exerted; so that the less shall not be sacrificed to the greater; nor the greater, slighting the less, arrogate, to its own injury, more than its due.

> (II, p. 432)

Judgement is the ground the poet shares with the reader. It is a patterning of human preferences, a realizing and exercizing of what are the real or desirable sympathies of mankind. On this ground the reader must take his independent stand. Poems come up to be understood by readers and poets to be judged. But the judgement works both ways. As we judge so are we judged. Ideally the reader should be the poet's equal (it was on a footing of equality Wordsworth wished the relation to be placed). He should be aware of the adequacies and inadequacies on either side. Readers, however, as Wordsworth observed with that minatory and admonitory zeal which invited the charge of egotism, are rarely ideal. Even apart from those who are 'too petulant to be passive to a genuine poet, and too feeble to grapple with him', readers on the whole are unlikely to measure up to the writer of importance. Though Wordsworth was aware of the possibility that he might himself be occasionally mistaken, he was even more aware of the chances that the reader would be much more so. The egotism is relentless and illuminating and justified:

I am sensible that my associations must have sometimes been particular instead of general, and that, consequently, giving to things a false importance, I may have sometimes written upon unworthy subjects; but I am less apprehensive on this account, than that my language may frequently have suffered from those arbitrary connections of feelings and ideas with particular words and phrases, from which no man can altogether protect himself. Hence I have no doubt, that, in some instances, feelings, even of the ludicrous, may be given to my Readers by expressions which appeared to me tender and pathetic. Such faulty expressions, were I convinced they were faulty at present, and that they must necessarily continue to be so, I would willingly take all reasonable pains to correct. But it is dangerous to make these alterations on the simple authority of a few individuals, or even of certain classes of men; for where the understanding of an Author is not convinced, or his feelings altered, this cannot be done without great injury to himself: for his own feelings are his stay and support; and, if he set them aside in one instance, he may be induced to repeat this act till his mind shall lose all confidence in itself, and become utterly debilitated. To this it may be added, that the Reader ought never to forget that he is exposed to the same errors as the Poet, and, perhaps, in a much greater degree: for there can be no presumption in saying of most readers, that it is not probable they will be so well acquainted with the various stages of meaning through which words have passed, or with the fickleness or stability of the relations of particular ideas to each other; and, above all, since they are so much less interested in the subject, they may decide lightly and carelessly.

(II, p. 402)

II

When a poet breaks with a way of writing he is also breaking, as Wordsworth said, with 'pre-established codes of decision'. Such a break pushes the poet at once into the region of the 'extrinsic'. His only recourse is to the simple and non-literary—or, rather, because no poet can be pushed outside the sphere of words, into modes of communication that are not part of the established codes: the poet might go back to a former tradition, or he might strive to create a new one. In asking readers to divest themselves of all their usual literary habits—habits which Wordsworth felt were in his time already degenerate and likely for various social reasons to deteriorate further—the poet is asking for a new naked-ness of relation. Of course the user of words cannot step out-side words. Nor can the 'man speaking to men' step outside what men know or are willing to be interested in. Simplicity, that is, sets up a much more 'general' context for communi-cation, and makes special because unprecedented demands on the reader. Wordsworth was queerly aware of this new relation. Writing of the new kind of poet he had in mind, he insisted:

> And you must love him e'er to you
> He will seem worthy of your love.

(IV, p. 67)

This awareness of the need for an initial indulgence is the obverse of the egotism which makes its peremptory demands in the *Advertisement*.

Breaking with 'pre-established codes of decision' and breaking with a literary language are the same thing: Words-worth objected as much to the matter of the eighteenth-century poet as to his manner, and was aware of a false cult of simplicity fashionable in his own time. To break into 'simplicity' meant rejecting the system whereby eighteenth-century poetry managed its internal verbal economy. Bare language will now have to carry the poem, mediating situation, and plot, and tone, until such time as the poet, creating the taste by which he will be appreciated, has established new habits in the reader, and opened a way for new intrinsic verbal relations (those, in Wordsworth's case, that have to do with 'coadunation') to be accepted as the norm of the poetic. The simplicity is an invitation to a new intimacy, a new discipline, and a new complexity. The rhythm of the revolutionary in literature—it is a sufficiently commonplace observation—is to break with the intrinsic, to call in the extrinsic, and thereafter gradually to develop new intrinsic codes, of symbol or diction, which are then handed on to the extenders or degenerators who follow.

Both Blake and Wordsworth illustrate the process of developing new intrinsicalities after an apparently anarchic rejection of what was received and current. Blake is the purer case, and we might illustrate again from *Songs of Innocence*.

'Infant Joy' is the extreme limit of 'simplicity'. To go further in this direction would be to transcend the literary medium altogether, as some 'silent poets', Wordsworth believed, did transcend it. But Blake was a literary genius as well as a genius. He successfully communicates. 'The Blossom', less bare than 'Infant Joy', shows the direction in which he moves to remain within the ring of words at all:

> Merry, merry sparrow!
> Under leaves so green,
> A Happy Blossom
> Sees you, swift as arrow,
> Seek your cradle narrow
> Near my bosom.
>
> Pretty, pretty Robin!
> Under leaves so green,

> A Happy Blossom
> Hears you sobbing, sobbing,
> Pretty, pretty Robin,
> Near my bosom.

The structure of the poem helps to sort out the meaning. The split into two verses suggests that a contrast or counter-poising of two types of behaviour is intended. The repetition-with-significant-variation ensures that the main points of the contrast will not be missed. Each verse contains the 'Happy Blossom' and the 'bosom', related in the first verse to a 'sparrow' and in the second to a 'robin'. The Blossom presides over the relationship between both the Girl and the Sparrow and the Girl and the Robin.

Traditionally, and in fact, the sparrow is common, greedy, aggressive, appetitive. The robin, like the sparrow a nursery-rhyme creature, is the opposite. It sits in a barn to keep itself warm and hides its head under its wing, poor thing. (Blake's originality here is to utilize common knowledge and the tradition of the nursery for the expression of most adult insights.) The Happy Blossom is fulfilment. The greenery is that of Spring, freshness and vitality. The Sparrow-Bosom relation is one of glad target-seeking and of equally glad acceptance. The Robin, on the other hand, can neither seek nor find self-fulfilment in mutuality. Yet the girl still takes it to her bosom.

By this time the meaning is well beyond what a nursery-rhyme usually contains, though still in touch with the level at which even children could get something from it which would neither be irrelevant nor a caricature. The sexual connotations, however, are obvious. The arrow is Cupid's, Blake's arrow of desire, and—so carelessly—a cliché rhyme with 'sparrow'. It is a male symbol, too, brought swiftly by its rhyme to the 'cradle narrow'. 'Cradle' is a strange word. It binds together the two great and sometimes wrongly opposed impulses. It unites the mistress and the mother in a single object. The sparrow is seeking not only its procreant

end but also its cosy beginning. The sparrow's appetite is a
need and also the answer to a need.

If the first verse celebrates passion and fulfilment the
second celebrates compassion and frustration. Blake, with
tremendous maturity, ratifies and accepts both. (D. H. Lawrence, on the whole, will have little patience with robins.)
For Blake the two attitudes together make up the systole and
diastole of the Divine-Human heart. Blake is sublimely un-
worried about 'love'. His poetry (maybe the greatest of
achievements) springs from a perfect absence of anxiety—
anxiety about his matter, his manner, himself, or his reader.

'The Blossom' is rooted firmly in the tradition of children's poetry, and in a common folk-imagery. To this extent
(like *Poetical Sketches*) it jumps out of one decorum into
another. We have maintained that 'simplicity' is difficult
in that it requires words to 'find' themselves so to speak in
very wide contexts: the context of words generally, of common experience generally, of the quality of a man generally
—a quality given in the large contours of his experience, his
decisions, ridge-and-valley-making choices, his set priorities,
his competence as a performer over the whole hazardous
terrain of risk and opportunity that life presents. A poet's
work will often construct a set of self-evincing symbols to
declare and indicate these contours. Different as the symbolism of *Songs of Innocence* is from that of the *Prophetic
Books*, it adequately carries the main Blake meanings. The
symbolism is geographical—a piece of late eighteenth-
century England. There are the green hills of eternity and
of the hymn-writers, with their sheep and their shepherd.
A river of instinctive energy and delight pours down from
these to the green pastures below. There the stream winds
past a village and a village-green, the oak-tree and the old
folk, through woods alive with children and birds, until
finally it reaches London. Here are mills, churches, ale-
houses, prisons, prostitutes, and soldiers, and the travesty of
regimented boys winding into St. Paul's 'like a river'. Each

of the Songs is a snapshot of this integral country. Blake successfully creates a symbolic context which will ultimately set up within itself the system of intrinsic cross-references necessary for full definition of meaning.

Wordsworth's simple poems and the 'experiments' of *Lyrical Ballads* resemble Blake's in important respects. Like Blake, Wordsworth requires his reader to forget his acquired literary habits—for his own sake:

> Readers accustomed to the gaudiness and inane phraseology of many modern writers, if they persist in reading this book to its conclusion, will perhaps frequently have to struggle with feelings of strangeness and awkwardness: they will look round for poetry, and will be induced to enquire by what species of courtesy these attempts can be permitted to assume that title. It is desirable that such readers, for their own sakes, should not suffer the solitary word Poetry, a word of very disputed meaning, to stand in the way of their gratification; but that, while they are perusing this book, they should ask themselves if it contains a natural delineation of human passions, human characters, human incidents; and if the answer be favourable to the author's wishes, that they should consent to be pleased in spite of that most dreadful enemy to our pleasures, our own pre-established codes of decision.
>
> (II, p. 383)

Like Blake, too, as we shall see, Wordsworth's poetic world develops its own set of intrinsic relationships. Symbolism— in any sense—is not Wordsworth's concern. Poetry for Wordsworth should purpose truth to life because it is life that is symbolic. Wordsworth's internal coherence therefore is seen in a system of habitual and recurrent concerns that outline the shape of a mind steadily busy with the shape of experiences and with those sorts of experiences that shape.

Less 'original' than Blake (Wordsworth suspects originality of being close to gaudy inanity) he wishes to speak as a man to men. He intends the restoration to their proper place of general human normalities. Verbally, he is less eccentric than Blake. Blake in *Poetical Sketches* had been only too sophisticated an assimilator and transformer of a forgotten Elizabethan past: 'Memory Hither Come' dissolves into itself the essences of *As You Like It* freshly perceived, two hundred years of love and melancholy in poetry, and adds furthermore its own personal overtones of acceptance and relinquishment—making melancholy a poised appraisal rather than a self-indulgent defeatism. Wordsworth's simple poems—as well as his blank verse—are more immediately relatable to previous forms of communication. Precursors of Wordsworth are misleadingly numerous: precursors in simplicity, in the ballad, and in blank-verse ruminations on God, Nature, Man and Society.

Wordsworth's characteristic 'simple' poem deals with less spectacular areas of experience than 'Infant Joy' or 'The Blossom'. Though less spectacular, Wordsworth however is no less real than Blake. Blake had written:

> How sweet is the Shepherd's sweet lot;
> From the morn to the evening he strays;
> He shall follow his sheep all the day;
> And his tongue shall be filled with praise.
>
> For he hears the lamb's innocent call,
> And he hears the ewes' tender reply;
> He is watchful while they are in peace,
> For they know that their Shepherd is nigh.

Wordsworth wrote (in 1797) 'The Reverie of Poor Susan', at first sight a characteristically affronting commonplace:

> At the corner of Wood Street, when daylight appears,
> Hangs a Thrush that sings loud, it has sung for three
>   years;
> Poor Susan has past by the spot and has heard
> In the silence of morning the song of the Bird.
>
> 'Tis a note of enchantment; what ails her? she sees
> A mountain ascending, a vision of trees;

Bright volumes of vapour through Lothbury glide,
And a river rolls on through the vale of Cheapside.

Green pastures she views in the midst of the vale
Down which she so often has tripped with her pail;
And a single small cottage, a nest like a dove's.
The one only dwelling on earth that she loves.

She looks and her heart is in heaven: but they fade,
The mist and the river, the hill and the shade:
The stream will not flow, and the hill will not rise,
And the colours have all past away from her eyes.

A lesser man writing this could easily have tumbled into
the insipid. Written a hundred years later it would begin and
end as merely a poetic over-valuation of nostalgia—like
Yeats's 'Lake Isle of Innisfree', for example. In the event
it is neither, and it is interesting to see how Wordsworth
brings it off.

First, the girl's situation is generalized by being closely
associated with the bird's. The girl and the thrush are
analogous cases. However, there is no heavy overload of
irony or pity: the thrush is a natural accident of the London
street touching off a natural feeling in the listener. The
casualness prepares us for the tone in which Susan will be
treated: there is sympathetic insight into her plight but no
identification with her feelings. This mingling of sympathy
and non-identification is clear in the second verse. The phrase
'bright volumes of vapour', with its slightly grandiloquent
alliteration, conjures up the swirl and swim of the girl's
dream but is already ironical. The river 'flows on through
the vale' only to come up against the external reality (to
which the poet is really more attentive) of Cheapside. The
last verse is a clever fusion of the two voices, that of poor
Susan herself, recognizing the hallucination for what it is,
and that of the poet inexorably overlaying the girl's: all such
hallucinations are transitory and unreal, it is the cage and
Cheapside that must be lived with:

31

She looks, and her heart is in heaven; but they fade,
The mist and the river, the hill and the shade;
The stream will not flow, and the hill will not rise;
And the colours have all past away from her eyes.

The poem is in fact not nostalgic, but an appreciation of what nostalgia means. It is about the thrush and the cage, and the country girl in London. It is about how poor servant-girls have their moments of home-sickness and impossible day-dream but must always come back to their poor servant-girls' lives. Wordsworth is not sentimental. He accepts the fact that the feeling exists but the feeling does not swamp his judgement. He neither identifies himself with the girl nor takes nostalgia for more (or less) than it is. Neither is the reader asked to identify himself with Susan: after all he does not share her situation. He is, however, asked to understand her and to share Wordsworth's perceptive sympathy and richly responding charity. Not to share these would be that form of sentimentality which does not feel for anything. The sharp contrast with Yeats's 'Lake Isle' in both these respects need not be underlined. Yeats *is* the nostalgic speaker, inviting identification with himself and with the mood. For Yeats the poetry is in the nostalgia. For Wordsworth the poetry is a response to the whole regrettable situation which forces up the pain of home-sickness, the illusory escape, and—for poor Susans—the even more painful return.

The experience organized in 'The Reverie of Poor Susan' is commonplace. But the commonplaces are not trivialities. The poem takes in the real or desirable sympathies of mankind. What is uncommon is the organization. The poem illustrates the broad-basedness of the Wordsworthian simplicity, and the range of the qualities that Wordsworth can bring together: the common decencies, sympathies, uncondescending indulgences, the Wordsworthian tenderness that is without fussiness and the toughness that is not insensitive —everything that Wordsworth relates to the centre of his design, both what he can admit to be real and what he knows also is desirable. Wordsworth's great source of strength and composure is his ability to admit the average into a total poetic frame of experience which never, at its best, remains merely ordinary.

We have inadvertently used the phrase 'poetic frame of experience'. We mean, of course, the structured consciousness of the poet himself. Simplicity of the Wordsworthian sort is achieved. Its spontaneous utterance is the expression of 'a man who, being possessed of more than usual organic sensibility, has also thought long and deeply'.

III

'The Reverie of Poor Susan' is an unpretentious example of Wordsworth's simplicity. Written before *Lyrical Ballads* it may indicate that the soil was ready for the seminal suggestion of the spring of 1798: that Wordsworth, with Coleridge, should write a volume of poems that would also be a literary manifesto.

We have claimed that 'simplicity' as a literary programme involves questions of considerable sophistication. We have brought from Wordsworth's *Prefaces* evidence that Wordsworth was aware of the nature of the problems concerned. The impression that grows is one of an alert and conscious artist, and of a consciousness pre-eminently literary-critical. The tone of the prefatory prose is formidably authoritative and confident. Particularly impressive is the awareness, to which the *Prefaces* witness, of the poet's knowledge as to what his task is in the contemporary situation.

Wordsworth was, as Blake was not, in the main post-Renaissance tradition. For Wordsworth the poet still had a responsibility to society. He was the spokesman and the guardian of social health. Or where health was departing from society it was the poet's duty to call society back, by example as much as by admonition. There is nothing that radically separates the Wordsworth who wrote the 'experiments' of *Lyrical Ballads* from the Wordsworth who wrote 'Milton, thou shouldst be living at this hour'—the literary revolutionary from the republican sonneteer. Maybe Wordsworth is the last great poet in the Renaissance tradition. After him comes Keats, and with Keats a decisive shift of poetic centre. With that shift comes a 'romanticism' Wordsworth would not very readily have been capable of sympathizing with, nor it with him. *Lyrical Ballads* at any rate was not taken up by the later nineteenth century as an integral part of the great romantic achievement. Yet Wordsworth, who held back *The Prelude* for posthumous publication, never ceased to regard *Lyrical Ballads* as containing some of his best work. Few—even among his admirers—enthusiastically agreed.

In the studies of the three most important 'lyrical ballads' that follow, Wordsworth's sophistication will be assumed at the start, sophistication of both motive and method. Of motive, for the reasons already argued. And of method, on the evidence of the poems themselves. A close reading of the ballads is necessary. Detailed examination brings out the subtlety of Wordsworth's innovations in technique and in procedural control. Wordsworth, to repeat, was not merely rejecting a certain vocabulary. From the start his achievement is positive. The 'experiments' were new and exciting literary explorations. All three poems belong to the Spring and early Summer of 1798.

II

THREE LYRICAL
BALLADS

W ordsworth called his lyrical ballads 'experiments'. I do not think, in so doing, he was apologizing for them. (He never went back on the judgement that *Lyrical Ballads* contained some of his best work.) Rather, he was drawing attention to the deliberateness of the venture, the probing into hitherto unexplored territory that *Lyrical Ballads* is. The deliberateness implies a certain sophistication also. The ballads, however simple, are never naïve. Some are much more successful than others. None of them is artlessly innocent 'expression'.

It is sometimes forgotten that Wordsworth's biggest work before *Lyrical Ballads* was not *The Evening Walk* or *Descriptive Sketches*, but *The Borderers*, a five-act blank-verse play. At the time of writing *Lyrical Ballads* Wordsworth was in fact as much a dramatist as a poet. Certainly, in most of the ballads there is an essentially dramatic self-projection. Wordsworth in this volume invents a new poetic form. The three poems to be considered are each of them, in different ways, *tours de force* in the dramatic-narrative technique which is the peculiarly Wordsworthian innovation of this time.

The lyrical ballad differs both from straightforward narrative, such as that of Crabbe, for example, and from dramatic monologue after the manner of Browning. Straight narrative assumes that the story is the important thing. The story-teller usually follows a standard convention, but whether the method is traditional or not the narrator himself must not be felt as interfering with the facts he is recording. Straight narrative will have its organizing controls somewhere in 'plot'. Dramatic monologue, on the other hand, finds its organizing centre somewhere in 'psychology' or 'character'. (It might go so far in this direction as to become the un-arranged 'stream of consciousness'.) The dramatic monologue exists to give away the character of the speaker. Curiously enough Wordsworth attempted to justify *The Thorn* by taking this line, though interest in the character of the retired sea-captain is the last thing that could explain the poem's permanent hold.

Wordsworth experiments with various mixtures of method in *Lyrical Ballads*. 'The Mad Mother' and 'The Complaint of the Forsaken Indian Woman' are first-person monologues, though not in any Browning sense dramatic. 'Goody Blake and Harry Gill', 'The Last of the Flock', and 'Anecdote for Fathers' approximate to straight narrative with a neutral narrator. The three poems we wish to concentrate on here are experiments in a more complex merging of the two methods—experiments in that mixed form in which Wordsworth found his first important opportunity.

Wordsworth seems to have had an exceptional ear for tones of voice. 'The Waggoner' (1802) is evidence of his ventriloquism. There the narrator's voice is replaced naturally by the Cumberland tones of the Waggoner himself or of an understanding Cumberland neighbour. We are constantly aware of the two levels. Wordsworth obtains his effect by modulating neither into dialect syntax nor vocabulary, but by reproducing the much subtler thing only a native ear could recognize—the vowel harmonies of the northern rhymes and word-sequences:

> The rain rushed down—the road was battered,
> As with the force of billows shattered;
> The horses are dismayed, nor know
> Whether they should stand or go;
> And Benjamin is groping near them,
> Sees nothing, and can scarcely hear them.
> He is astounded,—wonder not,—
> With such a charge in such a spot;
> Astounded in the mountain gap
> With thunder peals, clap after clap,
> Close-treading on the silent flashes—
> And somewhere, as he thinks, by crashes
> Among the rocks; with weight of rain,
> And sullen motions long and slow,
> That to a dreary distance go—
> Till, breaking in upon the dying strain,
> A rending o'er his head begins the fray again.
>
> (ll. 188–304)

All poets need to find their voice, or voices. Wordsworth began, as most do, with a voice not his own but belonging to the eighteenth century. *The Borderers* which followed closely on the early period may have opened out the possibilities of dramatic projection. In *Lyrical Ballads*, at any rate, Wordsworth has discovered his vehicle—the voice of the 'Statesman', or peasant small-holder, the voice of the retired sea-captain or West-country balladist; a literary personality that had not been used for serious purposes in this way before.

The mixed mode of the dramatic-narrative poem allows for a range of voices, and each voice for an ironic shift in point of view. It is unfortunate that Wordsworth's irony has not been much remarked. If irony, however, can mean perspective and the co-presence of alternatives, the refusal to impose on the reader a predigested life-view, the insistence on the contrary that the reader should enter, himself, as full partner in the final judgement on the facts set before him—then Wordsworth is a superb ironist in *Lyrical Ballads*. In the mixed mode of the poems the poet can take up and lay down his masks. And with each assumption or discard a new, sometimes excitingly dramatic, shift of standpoint is possible. The narrator, the characters involved in the story, the poet himself as the finally responsible assembler—these are the three main levels at which the voices work. By changing the voice one can step from one frame to another and back again. Stepping apparently out of the frame of mere 'literature' altogether and into the reader's own reality (his reality of experience and of judgement), confronting the reader with the need to be aware of what he is judging with as well as what he is judging—this is, above all, the Wordsworthian trick in *Lyrical Ballads*. 'Simon Lee' is an outstanding example of it. No wonder Wordsworth continued to stand by the poem as an example of his art at its subtlest, its least pretentious and plainest.

I

'Simon Lee' ends with the following lines:

> I've heard of hearts unkind, kind deeds
> With coldness still returning.
> Alas! the gratitude of men
> Has oftener left me mourning.

'Simon Lee' exists as a poem, I think, to carry these lines to the reader in the precise way it does: with the weight, the depth, the soberness, the measured seriousness and overflowing tenderness that they have. It exists, that is, to ensure the 'comprehensiveness in thinking and feeling' which Wordsworth thought the great poet should possess and the good reader acquire. How far Wordsworth has brought the reader in the poem can be gauged by the difference between these last four lines and the four lines with which the poem opens:

> In the sweet shire of Cardigan,
> Not far from pleasant Ivor-hall,
> An old man dwells, a little man,
> I've heard he once was tall.

As Wordsworth enters upon his task the pose he adopts is deceptive. Until the last lines are reached the poem throughout plays with ambiguities of tone. The reader is offered choices so various that he is chary—if he is sufficiently aware —of plumping for any one of the alternatives presented. Yet the various possibilities are pressed upon us, so that the suspension of choice has to be willed. We are the more resolved not to commit ourselves precipitately because of the feeling that the poet is up to something, because he is himself highly sophisticated, and because, we suspect, what he ultimately intends is nothing at all so obvious or so slight as what seems to be going on.

The alternatives in these first four lines are fairly apparent. Because of '*sweet* shire'—with its conventional adjective— we might be with the mannered revivalism of Percy's *Reliques*. 'Pleasant' too could be the expected ballad work, and there is 'pleasaunce' (a far echo) to give local ballad colour to the otherwise unassuming counter. The word as applied to Ivor-hall guarantees the reliability of the anonymous Everyman who might be presumed to be speaking. He is well-disposed, even to the Squire, certainly to the traditional sanctities of the established countryside. But the poem is not allowed to settle here. The two lines that follow present a sharp alternative: the extremes of burlesque (it might be) or of unconsciously funny sadbrow earnestness. In any case, that is, we step outside the straightforward convention into something less familiar:

> An old man dwells, a little man,
> I've heard he once was tall.

The ludicrous, if we like, is brought teasingly near the surface. It is as though the reader were being challenged to recognize his first impulse to laugh, get over it at the outset, and dismiss it for the rest of the poem. (How we read the poem depends on how we deal with these temptations which Wordsworth puts in our path.) That we do struggle with our frivolousness or indelicacy is due, I think, to the sense that we are being deliberately tempted. Wordsworth, we feel, is watching our reaction, neither helping nor hindering us from keeping our balance, but he is aware, balanced and immensely assured himself. We are checked by the knowledge that this is the writing of a man both sophisticated and serious-minded. Then, when we look at the lines again, there is actually nothing to laugh at. The prose-sense that Wordsworth can always release to such sobering effect comes up in full force. All that the lines now say is that near pleasant Ivor-hall,

> An old man dwells, a little man,
> I've heard he once was tall.

If the speaker were clowning the second line would be said with bumpkin obliviousness to the paradoxical 'little man . . . once was tall'. We should then be with the Albert-saga of Stanley Holloway. The temptation so to read it seems thrust forward, but is so obvious that it is easily overcome. And there is enough in the poem already to suggest sobriety. The opening lines, in fact, with their 'little man . . . tall' contradiction present only a small puzzle, and the solution of the puzzle throws up something at once realistic and pathetic. Read naturally, too, their whole tenour is against cheapness either way. Though the ballads are in mind, there are no mechanical ballad-metrics. There is a genuine and unaffected music in them, but it is a naturally singing dialect voice we hear—the regional voice of Wordsworth's Statesmen. Thus all four lines could be read with something of solemnity, and possibly the convinced Wordsworthian might prefer to take 'Simon Lee' throughout as a uniformly sober performance. This would not, however, be strictly conformable with the evidence. The tone of the poem is complicated with ironies. We have to reject the temptation to be sentimental as well as the temptation to laugh. The second half of the first stanza is deliberately intended to prevent a premature or misplaced seriousness. We have nothing as yet to be serious about:

> Of years he has upon his back,
> No doubt, a burthen weighty;
> He says he is three score and ten,
> But others say he's eighty.

The more jaunty movement, the apparently casual 'no doubt' (though it might mean, 'He certainly is *very* old, and no mistake!'), the 'He says—others say' pit-pat, the flightiness and near-jocularity of the concluding feminine rhyme (the sound of the word clashing ironically with the sense)—all this makes over-earnestness impossible. Of set purpose Wordsworth is interested in keeping the emotional temperature down, and the reader in suspense.

The movement towards full seriousness of tone in this first part is expertly managed. The delicacy of the shift is maybe better suggested by a reading-aloud than by an analysis such as we are attempting. (The danger in piecemeal exposition is that the passages isolated from their context might collapse back on the burlesque or the banal or the solemn, the very thing the subtle normalities and the freshness of the poem are designed to avoid.) However, something of what Wordsworth is doing can be focused on in his use of language. There is a significant repetition, for example, of operative words and phrases, repetitions with new increments of meaning. Thus, the sequence 'old-poor—poor old' is used twice. The first 'old' is in the lines already quoted concerning the 'old man'. The word 'poor' occurs in the verse following:

> A long blue livery-coat has he,
> That's fair behind, and fair before;
> Yet, meet him where you will, you see
> At once that he is poor.

The two words are combined in the next verses:

> His hunting feats have him bereft
> Of his right eye, as you may see;
> And then, what limbs those feats have left
> To poor old Simon Lee!

The sequence occurs a second time in the verses that move up to the climax of the first part:

> Old Ruth works out of doors with him,
> And does what Simon cannot do.
>
> A scrap of land they have, but they
> Are poorest of the poor.
>
> Few months of life has he in store,
> As he to you will tell,
> For still, the more he works, the more
> His poor old ancles swell.

The progress in each case is through the matter-of-fact senses of 'old' and 'poor' to the indulgently sympathetic. Age and poverty are first coolly seen as fact, and it is only then that the natural and appropriate concern for them is invited. A similar procedure is followed with the word 'little': first, 'a little man', the scientific sense predominating and then the frankly tender diminutive:

> And he is lean, and he is sick,
> His little body's all awry;
> His ancles they are swoln and thick:
> His legs are thin and dry.

One of the most telling repetions is the second reference to Ivor-hall:

His master's dead, and no one now
Dwells in the hall of Ivor;
Men, dogs, and horses, all are dead,
He is the sole survivor.

The 'hall of Ivor' sounds grim and mockingly sardonic. The high-flownness of the phrase contrasts with the devastation and down-in-the-worldness the lines tell us about. The literariness, too, adds its point: it recalls violently the opposed associations of 'pleasant Ivor-hall', so that the levelling jacobinism of Time (the reality) echoes ironically against the toryism (the pretence) of the first and merely 'literary' form. In this third verse a new sombreness of tone and subject is reached:

Men, dogs, and horses, all are dead

—the heavy monosyllables beat it out.

Wordsworth frames the personal tragedy of infirmity and poverty in the larger social tragedy of the decaying countryside. Throughout the first part, in fact, the dealings of Time with Man are concretely presented in social and personal terms together. The livery the old man wears reminds us of his former status as well as of his one-time vigour. Its out-of-placeness is two-fold, bringing home the pathos of the vanished security and the punyness of the form that can no longer fill it. Other details interchangeably suggest the private and the public worlds and the corrosion at work in each: the plot of ground enclosed 'from the heath', and Simon's being '*forced* to work, though weak'. By the end of this first part a whole era of social decay as well as personal decline has been suggested. At the end, such is Wordsworth's certainty that we are with him on his own terms, and are divested of our habitual notions concerning what is fit to be mentioned in poetry, that he risks his main, most confident, and most daring repetition—Simon's culminating infirmity, the scandalous particularity of the swollen ankles:

43

> Few months of life has he in store,
> As he to you will tell,
> For still, the more he works, the more
> His poor old ancles swell.

We are no longer listening to words as literature; we are listening to literature only as it can use words to present the significant facts. We want only the truth and 'comprehensiveness of thinking and feeling'.

Having forced the admission into poetry of such words and things as poor old ankles, Wordsworth turns (the moment is almost slily calculated) to apostrophize the reader:

> My gentle reader, I perceive
> How patiently you've waited,
> And I'm afraid that you expect
> Some tale will be related.
> O reader! had you in your mind
> Such stores as silent thought can bring,
> O gentle reader! you would find
> A tale in everything.
> What more I have to say is short,
> I hope you'll kindly take it;
> It is no tale, but should you think
> Perhaps a tale you'll make it.

The word 'gentle' is interestingly weighted. There is first the sense of 'submissive, amenable', and the condescension implied. There is also the opposite meaning, as in 'gentle and simple': 'well-born, polished and sophisticated, high in station'. The ambivalence reminds us of the reversible attitudes entertained to Ivor-Hall, of the poet as ballad-retainer, and the poet as natural aristocrat. Underlying the two opposites and alternatives is the reconciling democratic meaning. To be gentle is to be tenderly considerate of others, willing to suffer them and suffer with them, to cherish and forbear—the feeling that equalizes inevitable inequalities and establishes the true fraternity. This is almost the basic

meaning here. The reversibility of the superior-inferior relation makes possible a new kind of mutuality, an *equality* if we
wish to use the word, but an equality that stands not on
rightful demands so much as on reciprocal indulgences. This
basic meaning of 'gentle' is supported by 'patiently' in the
next line. To be patient is to submit, but the submission is
from strength, as we might be patient in a storm, or with a
child. In this instance the patience is ascribed to the Reader,
not adopted by the Poet. Thus, in the twelve lines of the
apostrophe, we are swung through the whole range of the
not mutually exclusive attitudes involved, from that of indul-
gent patron to that of sturdy but deferential countryman:

> What more I have to say is short,
> I hope you'll kindly take it.

Wordsworth accurately catches the note of the peasant voice.
He demonstrates too his command of 'the common word
precise': here, the word 'kindly'—as belongs to man*kind*,
with the *kind*ness we ought to have, and really do have at
bottom: once we have reached bottom and discovered our
kind.

   This second movement unites writer and reader very inti-
mately and yet leaves each remarkably independent. Within
the relationship thus established a fuller 'comprehensiveness' is possible. The third part is now prepared for: the
incident of the wood-cutting. Wordsworth tells the story
with matter-of-fact faithfulness and even with a trace of
humour. Simon's futility is pitiable but also laughable:
naturally so to a young man who is himself firm and hearty
and who knows he has age yet to come to:

> One summer day I chanced to see
> This old man doing all he could
> About the root of an old tree,
> A stump of rotten wood.
> The mattock totter'd in his hand;
> So vain was his endeavour

That at the root of the old tree
He might have worked for ever.

'You're overtasked, good Simon Lee,
Give me your tool,' to him I said;
And at the word right gladly he
Receiv'd the proffer'd aid.
I struck, and with a single blow
The tangled root I sever'd,
At which the poor old man so long
And vainly had endeavour'd.

The ordinary tone is essential to the meaning. There is nothing extraordinary in Simon Lee's age and poverty. The impulse to lend him a hand is also perfectly natural. To call attention to it with undue emphasis would be to over-stress the common stuff of human nature that is so easily, so promptly, and yet so casually being brought into play. The great deepening of tone comes in the climax of the last verse:

The tears into his eyes were brought,
And thanks and praises seemed to run
So fast out of his heart, I thought
They never would have done.
—I've heard of hearts unkind, kind deeds
With coldness still returning.
Alas! the gratitude of men
Has oftener left me mourning.

'I've heard of hearts unkind'—we can hear the weariness, the impatience amounting to contempt, in Wordsworth's voice. He is conjuring up the whole sickening sphere of the moral and verbal cliché, the set-pieces of life and literature, the jejune dogmas that encase the mind, hardening it into impercipience or indifference. The literary 'winter wind' is never really *too* unkind—especially to the arrogant self-righteousness it can so often subserve. The Jaques mentality, however, is as far from the Wordsworthian comprehensiveness as Arden is from the enclosed bit of heath and mossed cottage of Simon Lee. Moral emphases of a profound range and depth and normality are being redistributed as we read. The poet, as he later will say, has placed us 'in the way of receiving from ordinary moral sensations another and more salutary impression than we are accustomed to receive from them'.

The paradox of the final two lines is not a merely verbal trick, like the Oscar Wilde inversion of commonplaces. And the reader is left to interpret its fullness as he best can. Through the course of the poem, but culminating here, Wordsworth has effected his literary and psychic re-education. The reader is restored to independence: independence of the 'poetic', and independence (a more difficult thing) of the Poet—of the writer, that is, as the provider of new 'attitudes to life', of novel patterns and formulae of response. He is restored to himself, to that fresh air which he shares with the poet and with all men but which he must breathe for himself. What, for example, we might be moved to press on the poet, what is there in 'gratitude' to lead to 'mourning'? But what in a case like this can the poet tell us that we don't know already, and that his poem has not already put us in the way to realize? The answer might include reference to the iniquities of society and the harshness of Time in its dealings with men. Both these references the poem makes. What mourning is it, though, that supervenes on the young man's vigorous health and good spirits, and goes even deeper than the tears that are brought to the eyes of a helpless old man? The question is best left rhetorical. Answers here might themselves remain mere rhetoric: such rhetoric as,

> The still, sad music of humanity

or even,

> Thoughts that do often lie too deep for tears.

The mourning becomes a Wordsworthian negative that seems immensely positive in its secure power, its capacity to feel the hurt and yet to embrace the hurtful.

II

THE IDIOT BOY

Apart from Hutchinson and Dowden few people have thought of Wordsworth as a comic poet. Yet it is clear that in *Lyrical Ballads* Wordsworth, in some of his most successful poems, is writing in a humorous vein. Hutchinson's note is fairly dismissive:

> The humour and pathos of *The Idiot Boy* are sadly marred by his clumsy attempts at mirth. Hazlitt, in his pen-portrait of Wordsworth, speaks of a certain 'convulsive inclination to laughter about the mouth, a good deal at variance with the solemn, stately expression of the rest of his face'. Not less awkward and incongruous, surely, are the heavy pleasantries in which the poet of *Peter Bell* and *The Idiot Boy* seeks an occasional vent for his exuberant cheerfulness. 'At rare times in his poetry Wordsworth shows an inclination for frolic: it is the frolic of good spirits in the habitually grave, and he cannot caper lightly and gracefully.'

One has to bear in mind, of course, that for the nineteenth-century critic serious poetry could not be both serious and comic at the same time. One has also to bear in mind, in justice to the commentators, that on the whole serious Wordsworthian comedy is rare. There is, however, the testimony of *Lyrical Ballads*, and the undeniable evidence of the introduction to 'Peter Bell', which belongs to the same period.

'The Thorn' and 'The Idiot Boy' were Wordsworth's own favourites in the *Lyrical Ballads* volume. And Wordsworth may have been right. He was a mature twenty-seven, the volume was a sophisticated experiment as well as a revolutionary manifesto, and the poet had clear ideas as to what he was doing.

From the start of the poem we are aware of the distinctive narrating voice, and of the narrator's power to merge his own voice in that of the actors in the story, as well as of his

capacity to re-emerge when necessary and regain his com-
menting distinctness. The story-teller is near enough in
social status to Betty Foy to have ready and sympathetic
insight into the working of her mind. At the same time he is
not in her shoes. He does not share either her concern or her
simple-mindedness. He is, however, in every sense, a good
neighbour. The mergence of his voice with his neighbours
is all the easier because he has the same village language, and
the outlook that goes with it:

> 'Tis eight o'clock—a clear March night,
> The moon is up—the sky is blue,
> The owlet in the moonlight air,
> He shouts from nobody knows where;
> He lengthens out his lonely shout,
> Halloo! halloo! a long halloo!
>
> —Why bustle thus about your door,
> What means this bustle, Betty Foy?
> Why are you in this mighty fret?
> And why on horseback have you set
> Him whom you love, your idiot boy?
>
> Beneath the moon that shines so bright,
> Till she is tired, let Betty Foy
> With girth and stirrup fiddle-faddle;
> But wherefore set upon a saddle
> Him whom she loves, her idiot boy?

The voice expresses surprise, impatience, and some dis-
approval. The observer is neither an idiot, nor a silly
woman: 'fiddle-faddle' carries its own comment on the fussy
confusion of Betty's muddledness and misplaced pride, and
on the womanish clumsiness with 'girth and stirrup'—those
traditionally masculine implements of management and control. But, once the silliness might really lead to serious consequences, the observer can easily slip into Betty's and Susan's
situation:

> Poor Susan moans, poor Susan groans,
> 'As sure as there's a moon in heaven,'
> Cries Betty, 'he'll be back again;
> They'll both be here, 'tis almost ten,
> They'll both be here before eleven!'

He can even assume the point of view of the pony, which is included in the same comprehensive sentence, and awarded in the poem a wisdom and dignity of its own:

> But then he is a horse that thinks!
> But when he thinks his pace is slack;
> Now, though he knows poor Johnny well,
> Yet for his life he cannot tell
> What he has got upon his back.

The tone is beautifully mock-solemn and yet indulgently ready with its sympathy. We are encouraged to take the other's point of view, but not allowed to forget the observer's. It is not a dismissive fun, nor the detachment of aloofness. The superiority is also a magnanimity. We are called on for tenderness rather than condescension: but not to surrender our own identity. Wordsworth's peculiar achievement is an irony of detachment and loving-kindness.

It is Wordsworth himself, of course, who is the narrator, and he makes us aware of his masks. Dropping the rôle of merged narrator he steps in front of the curtain when Betty's anxiety has reached its climax. The timing is perfect—and so is the surprise: the irony that is now turned on the reader himself:

> Oh reader! now that I might tell
> What Johnny and his horse are doing!
> What they've been doing all this time,
> Oh could I put it into rhyme,
> A most delightful tale pursuing!
>
> Perhaps, and no unlikely thought!
> He with his pony now doth roam
> The cliffs and peaks so high that are,

To lay his hands upon a star,
And in his pocket bring it home.

Perhaps he's turned himself about,
His face unto his horse's tail,
And still and mute, in wonder lost,
All like a silent horseman-ghost,
He travels on along the vale.

And now, perhaps, he's hunting sheep,
A fierce and dreadful hunter he!
Yon valley, that's so trim and green,
In five month's time, should he be seen,
A desert wilderness will be.

Perhaps, with head and heels on fire,
And like the very soul of evil,
He's galloping away, away,
And so he'll gallop on for aye,
The bane of all that dread the devil.

I to the Muses have been bound,
These fourteen years, by strong indentures;
Oh gentle muses! let me tell
But half of what to him befel,
For sure he met with strange adventures.

Oh gentle Muses! is this kind?
Why will ye thus my suit repel?
Why of your further aid bereave me?
And can ye thus unfriended leave me?
Ye muses! whom I love so well.

The irony turns against the reader. The reader wants mar-
vels? Wordsworth will hold up a screen on which he can
project his own. They are terribly stale literary stock—the
sublimely whimsical, the Monk Lewis, the Quixotic; mad
Ajaxes and romantic wild-men. Wordsworth conjures up the
fancies in order to indulge so many reading-public weak-

nesses, and, again, detach himself from them. But as ne can tolerate the silliness he can cater for the vacuity. The equable rebuke, however, or warning, is implicit in his manner all the time. The simpleton-narrator uses his folly as a stalking horse. This is the point in the poem (a point occurring, too, in 'Simon Lee' and 'The Thorn') of the defecation of the 'literary'. Betty finds Johnny safe. On their return home Susan is better. When Johnny is asked how he spent his time, his reply is the idiotic verse which set Wordsworth off writing the poem:

> 'The cocks did crow to-whoo, to-whoo,
> And the sun did shine so cold.'
> —Thus answered Johnny in his glory,
> And that was all his travel's story.

'The Idiot Boy' is a comedy, though admittedly a Wordsworthian comedy. The story has mock-epic features: a life-and-death issue; the last chance of success depending on the last person likely to succeed; mental conflict between mother-love and good-neighbourliness; the anguished search and rescue of the rescuer; finally, the happy issue out of everyone's afflictions, Susan's included. At times Wordsworth's management of stanza and rhyme can remind us of the professional humourist:

> Long Susan lay deep lost in thought,
> And many dreadful fears beset her,
> Both for her messenger and nurse;
> And as her mind grew worse and worse,
> Her body it grew better.

That is at least as good as Tom Hood, but instead of the merely local pun on a word there is a kind of story-pun: Betty having gone off after Johnny, Susan catches a cumulative anxiety for them both. There is also the sane psychology as well as the joke, and the moral implied: Susan is cured of her psychological bed-riddenness by an honest and maybe unwonted care for others. Generosity rallies to the aid of generosity. The fun never falls outside Wordsworth's major convictions concerning what being human entails.

Wordsworth is capable also however of a comic vision that points more to his eighteenth-century origin than to his mid-Victorian destination. There is, for example, the encounter with the Doctor:

> And now she's at the doctor's door,
> She lifts the knocker, rap, rap, rap;
> The doctor at the casement shews
> His glimmering eyes that peep and doze;
> And one hand rubs his old night-cap.
>
> 'Oh Doctor! Doctor! where's my Johnny?'
> 'I'm here, what is't you want with me?'
> 'Oh Sir! you know I'm Betty Foy,
> 'And I have lost my poor dear boy,
> 'You know him—him you often see;
>
> 'He's not so wise as some folk be.'
> 'The devil take his wisdom!' said
> The Doctor, looking somewhat grim,
> 'What, woman! should I know of him?'
> And, grumbling, he went back to bed.

There is nothing here of the clumsy frolic Dowden objected to. The social observation is swift and accurate. The rattling comic tempo is perfectly maintained. Everything happens in character, and the best joke is one that Wordsworth doesn't labour:

> 'Oh Doctor! Doctor! where's my Johnny?'
> 'I'm here, what is't you want with me?'

Wordsworth displays great tact in not underlining his jokes. It is obvious, for example, that Betty should have carried Johnny's message to the Doctor: that she forgot is part of the comedy. Wordsworth, however, at this point, is willing to let the joke look after itself. He is more concerned to preserve the proportion between joke and seriousness that his

53

poem requires. With all the comedy we are reminded that Betty is genuinely upset, and that Wordsworth has a sincere regard for her capacity to care.

It is most important to remember the seriousness that embraces the comic in Wordsworth's achievement. Wordsworth's irony, we have said, is an irony of detachment and loving-kindness. His comedy, too, requires us to overcome the taboo on tenderness. From Jonson onwards literary laughter had had to be punitive and corrective. Wordsworth asks us to understand (which implies detachment) and to forgive (which implies engagement). He neither scorns nor sentimentalizes the actors in his story. And, in fact, none of the emotions woven into the plot are mean or reprehensible. Susan is a neighbour really in distress. Betty Foy is a mother and a neighbour really attempting something noble whichever way the situation throws her. Her fiddle-faddle and infatuation may be both silly and risky, but neither is contemptible. Her anguished anxiety also is only laughable if our laughter has the Wordsworthian correlative: if we would be as ready to relieve it as to point out its (eventually to be made apparent) unnecessariness.

There is an essential poignancy and idiocy in emotion itself. Only the final upshot can decide which aspect will come uppermost. The great comedy of 'The Idiot Boy', quite apart from its surface jokes, has to do with this: it is a comedy of the passions. Far from being another Man of Feeling Wordsworth, in this poem, is the satirist of feeling. Betty's access of concern for Susan makes her send Johnny off on the errand. Fatuously she sees her idiot son as public hero. When he does not return, fear for his safety brings her back to the facts, and dispels neighbourly concern—and so on. And, as we have already hinted, the pattern is repeated in Susan, too. Her mysterious illness vanishes as she frets more and more about the others. Finally she is cured of imaginary illness by real emotional distress. Passions spin the plot—but arbitrarily. The idiocy of passion can precipitate its puppets into irrational misery or unpredictable joy. It all depends, but the dependence is not on the actors in the story as prudent agents. Man, as mere man of feeling, sits on a crazy see-saw.

The Idiot Boy himself, of course, gives still another dimension. The Idiot is not on the see-saw of passion. This means, from one point of view, he will escape its particular kinds of silliness. Wordsworth is fully aware of the Divine Fool archetype he is using. In his letter to Wilson (1802) he wrote

> *I have often applied to idiots, in my own mind, that sublime expression of Scripture that Their Life is Hidden with God.* They are worshipped, probably from a feeling of this sort, in several parts of the East ... I have, indeed, often looked upon the conduct of parents, in the lower ranks of society, toward idiots as a great triumph of the human heart. *It is there that we see the strength, disinterestedness, and grandeur of love;* nor have I ever been able to contemplate an object that calls out so many excellent and virtuous sentiments without finding it hallowed thereby, and having something in one which bears down before it like a deluge every feeble sensation of disgust and aversion.

The primitive force of the symbol exerts itself throughout the poem. Johnny has a dual rôle. He cannot be responsible for his actions, and it is his failure to fetch the doctor that is more effective than his mother's concern for her neighbour. That is the comic side. The divine is suggested not only through 'the strength, the disinterestedness, and the grandeur of love' he evokes in Betty and Susan (though not in the doctor), but also in the invulnerability of the joy that goes with him, an inaccessible but real emotion, the incomprehensible but mysteriously meaningful dialogue in which he takes part:

> Burr, burr—now Johnny's lips they burr,
> As loud as any mill, or near it,
> Meek as a lamb the pony moves,
> And Johnny makes the noise he loves,
> And Betty listens, glad to hear it.

> Away she hies to Susan Gale:
> And Johnny's in a merry tune,
> The owlets hoot, the owlets curr,
> And Johnny's lips they burr, burr, burr,
> And on he goes beneath the moon.

It would be easy to exaggerate this side of the Idiot in the poem. He is there, certainly, however, as an indication of the possibility of other dimensions, worlds unrealized that may be realizable. But Wordsworth does not make him more than a token of the possibilities. More important for the Wordsworthian seriousness of the tale is the Wordsworthian background into which Johnny is merged: the pony 'meek as a lamb', the moon, the river and waterfall, the whole natural universe that comes to life at the moments of greatest human stress or distraction:

> She listens, but she cannot hear
> The foot of horse, the voice of man;
> The streams with softest sound are flowing,
> The grass you almost hear it growing,
> You hear it now if e'er you can.

> The owlets through the long blue night
> Are shouting to each other still:
> Fond lovers, yet not quite hob nob,
> They lengthen out the tremulous sob,
> That echoes far from hill to hill.

It is the background which incarnates all the values the human world does not; energy and calm, permanence and process, spontaneity and order, ranging from the stars in the sky to the nearby birds:

> By this the stars were almost gone,
> The moon was setting on the hill,
> So pale you hardly looked at her:
> The little birds began to stir,
> Though yet their tongues were still.

Johnny is shut out from the various harmony of this order as inevitably as he is excluded from the confusions of the human order. Where the Idiot is concerned, Wordsworth is a realist:

> Of moon or stars he takes no heed:
> Of such we in romances read.

That is why we are left with Johnny's mad remark at the end:

> 'The cocks did crow to-whoo, to-whoo,
> And the sun did shine so cold.'

The Idiot has an insulated joy; Betty and Susan the confined, pitiful vulnerability of conflicting compassions; the Doctor sullenly slams the window on both. Nowhere in the human sphere is there the massive and potent integration of force, serenity, and tenderness, we find in the world of the waterfall, moon, and owls. The comedy, then, has its sombre side.

The especially poignant thing about the happy ending is its chance-givenness. Wordsworth will need, ultimately a third position beyond the dilemma which both 'The Thorn' and 'The Idiot Boy' leave him with. For Martha Ray and the Idiot Boy are the two horns of a dilemma. In spite of their surface differences in mood and in conclusion, the two poems agree that feeling, as feeling, is a kind of unhingement. The alienation of the normal which we see in 'The Idiot Boy' might be an even more pessimistic vision than that of 'The Thorn': for Martha's tragedy can be regarded, mitigably, as exceptional and personal. Betty's and Susan's, and the Doctor's, on the other hand is the alienation of the everyday and general. From this, complete idiocy is the only escape, unless an ultimate marriage of human mind and natural order might somehow and somewhere be possible.

III

THE THORN

To be better understood Wordsworth thought this poem needed an introductory preface. The preface, no doubt, would have been similar to that of 'Peter Bell'. It would have introduced the narrator and set his stage. We should have entered into his circumstances and become accustomed to his tone of voice. Preliminary acquaintance with the speaker's capacities and shortcomings would have guided the reader in supplying the *intelligiturs* of his story.

In 'The Thorn' Wordsworth had a surprisingly specific narrator in mind. When we read the note of 1800 he seems individualized to the point of near irrelevance:

> This Poem ought to have been preceded by an introductory Poem. . . . The character which I have here introduced speaking is sufficiently common. The Reader will perhaps have a general notion of it, if he has ever known a man, a Captain of a small trading vessel, for example, who being past the middle age of life, had retired upon an annuity or small independent income to some village or country town of which he was not a native, or in which he had not been accustomed to live. Such men, having little to do, become credulous and talkative from indolence; and from the same cause, and other predisposing causes by which it is probable that such men may have been affected, they are prone to superstition. On which account it appeared to me proper to select a character like this to exhibit some of the general laws by which superstition acts upon the mind. (II, p. 512)

Wordsworth's defensive rationalization of the intention behind the poem takes him a long way. For the knowledgeable reader, the main interest, it is suggested, will be the psychology of the narrator. Actually, of course, nothing could be more misleading. The narrator's rôle is important for transmitting the total experience of the poem. And the effect of the narration depends directly in part on our sense of what kind of person is speaking. But, as a reading will demonstrate, it is what the narrator says, as well as who he is and what he is like, that is important. Wordsworth uses his narrator imaginatively as the main regulator and director of our sympathies. He is, however, a means to the poem not an end in himself.

As it stands, then, the poem lacks any sort of prologue or preparation. The reader is plunged *in medias res*. Significantly, Wordsworth begins with the natural-symbolic setting and not with the story itself:

> There is a thorn; it looks so old,
> In truth you'd find it hard to say,
> How it could ever have been young,
> It looks so old and grey.
> Not higher than a two-years' child,
> It stands erect this aged thorn;
> No leaves it has, no thorny points;
> It is a mass of knotted joints,
> A wretched thing forlorn.
> It stands erect, and like a stone
> With lichens it is overgrown.

What sort of a speaker do the first seven stanzas insist upon? He is a man not given to intellectualizing his experiences. He pretends to no adjectival nicety or novelty of discrimination in his account. His epithets are both limited and broad, limited in number, broad in their folk-obviousness or literary jejuneness. Yet on occasion they can be strangely rich as well as common in the attitudes they draw upon and organize:

> And this poor thorn they clasp it round . . .
> To bury this poor thorn for ever.

Poor is the common folk-usage. The thorn is a poor thing beneath anyone's normal attention or consideration. Therefore it calls on compassion—provided we have an overplus of compassion to bestow: for the *poor* are too aware of their insignificance to claim this sort of attention. They are both too humble and too noble to beg. All the more therefore ought we to give freely, as an act of magnanimity and as an act of homage too. We who give are inferior to the objects of our compassion: we have not been called upon to endure so much, have not proved that we are beyond and above the expectation of sympathy. So only the poor can afford to call each other poor: the word expresses a common dignity and a common plight.

It is from something of this hinterland of broad folk attitudes that the speaker emerges. And it is from Words-worth's instinct for this sort of meaningful complexity in the uses of the common word that his simple poems derive their resonance as well as their reality. But the speaker in the poem is not himself a professional literary man. He is not even a country singer (as the narrator might be in 'Simon Lee'). When he ventures the literary turn he has a fatal fondness for *cliché*, though the clumsy juxtaposition of high-falutin' and crude guarantees that nothing in the narrative is being faked that we don't at once know about:

> And close beside this aged thorn,
> There is a fresh and lovely sight,
> A *beauteous heap*—

Wordsworth takes us up to the top of the literary-sentimental stairs in order to bump us down on the missing step of *heap*. Whenever the narrator ventures on to the field of sensibility he is uncertain. He elaborates on the 'heap', for example, and the dramatic irony is at once apparent:

> All lovely colours there you see,
> All colours that were ever seen,
> And mossy network too is there,
> As if by hand of lady fair
> The work had woven been,
> And cups, the darlings of the eye,
> So deep is their vermilion dye.
>
> Ah me! What lovely tints are there!
> Of olive-green and scarlet bright,
> In spikes, in branches, and in stars,
> Green, red, and pearly white.
> This heap of earth o'ergrown with moss,
> Which close beside the thorn you see,

> So fresh in all its beauteous dyes,
> Is like an infant's grave in size
> As like as like can be:
> But never, never any where
> An infant's grave was half so fair.

The mound is grotesquely prettified in order that what is said should echo gruesomely against what might be feared or suggested. There is a whole series of displacements, for a Wordsworthian poem: the praise of nature by comparing it to needlework, of the simple by making it an effort to out-do the high-society, and most of all (if we are meant to understand that this cannot be an infant's grave) the disadvantageous comparison of children's graves, aesthetically, with this particularly embroidered mound. But the speaker, as literary entrepreneur, is a failure—except that his failures mediate poetic ironies. In his own right he is a common man set in the midst of facts, and among the communal fancies of his neighbours that are also facts, facts he cannot reflect upon, nor, from talkativeness and a direct sense of the extraordinary, refrain from imparting. He is repetitive. His reiterations are almost obsessive. But as a witness he is reliable. He does not for his own part claim to have any significant feelings. He is merely one stubborn phenomenon testifying to the existence of others:

> Not five yards from the mountain-path,
> This thorn you on your left espy;
> And to the left, three yards beyond,
> You see a little muddy pond
> Of water, never dry;
> I've measured it from side to side:
> 'Tis three feet long, and two feet wide.

The impression of the fully-realized person who owns the narrative-voice is essential to the poem's success. At the lowest level the poem does dramatize a particular speaker. Yet obviously Wordsworth was wrong to put the poem forward only as an illustration of how a man 'past the middle age of life . . . can exhibit some of the general laws by which superstition acts upon the mind'. The narrator exists to mediate something more complex than this. He is merely a device whereby the varying flow of our experience is controlled.

Not all that the narrator says presses forward the question of his dramatic personality as a small ship's-captain. From another side, the narrator is representative unsophisticated man. As such he faces away from the narrowly social. He is a medium for the elemental in the human situation, the elemental in human beings themselves, and the elemental in those conditions they might at times be called to face. On this side his voice can blend with the Wordsworthian proper. At the end of the first movement of 'The Thorn', after attention has been compulsively focused on the stunted bush itself, on the muddy pond, and the grave-like hill of moss, we are brought face to face with the central human figure in the story, the crazy and bereaved creature who might be both a mother and a murderess:

> Now would you see this aged thorn,
> This pond and beauteous hill of moss,
> You must take care to chuse your time
> The mountains when to cross.
> For oft there sits, between the heap
> That's like an infant's grave in size,
> And that same pond of which I spoke,
> A woman in a scarlet cloak,
> And to herself she cries,
> 'Oh misery! oh misery!
> Oh woe is me! oh misery!'

We are approaching the climax of the first movement, and it is powerfully and skilfully managed. Wordsworth has already accustomed us to the pattern of repetition in his verse. The repetition has served to characterize the speaker. It has cunningly produced also an almost hypnotic effect, making us nightmarishly aware of 'things' as Things, things existing in their own dominating right, escaping the adjectival categories of consciousness. Now the repetition exerts its maximum force. The woman is first related to the three things of the setting, then (suddenly) to a wider Wordsworthian context of day and night, wind and stillness, sky and stars:

> At all times of the day and night
> This wretched woman thither goes,
> And she is known to every star,
> And every wind that blows;
> And there beside the thorn she sits
> When the blue day-light's in the skies,
> And when the whirlwind's on the hill,
> And frosty air is keen and still,
> And to herself she cries,
> 'Oh misery! oh misery!
> Oh woe is me! oh misery!'

The items of the setting and the protagonist in the tragedy have been so mediated to us through the voice of the narrator (now an ordinary 'Captain of a small trading vessel', now the representative of simple-and-universal) that facts take on the force of symbol. And, indeed, each of the main agents in the poem can be readily established as part of the Wordsworthian poetic universe—a seemingly inverted Wordsworthianism, it is true, because as yet Wordsworth has not arrived at the phase which will later be taken as 'typical' of him, and which the nineteenth century will ratify as official: the Wordsworth of the placid pool mirroring the quiet sky, the Wordsworth of the unstunted tree, the Wordsworth who will insist on joy as the bond between man and his natural environment, the 'grand principle of pleasure'. Here there is no

> stream as clear as sky
> When earth and heaven do make one imagery.

(I, p. 247)

We get instead the little muddy pond, narrowly constricted within its mathematically known dimensions. And the thorn-bush we have already encountered in the spine-chilling comparison of the first verse (a thing exactly companionable to the shuddering pond)—

> so old and grey,
> Not higher than a two-years' child

The juxtaposition in the comparison was unusual. It can now be recognized as deliberately premonitory—this eerie conjunction of dwarfed decreptitude and the two-years' child, all intervening growth, maturity, and decline omitted, and the potential of life put suddenly alongside what its promise will come to and might as well already be: gnarled, deformed, unresponsive age, the Thorn 'like a stone'.

'But in a poem', Coleridge wrote, 'still more in a lyric poem . . . it is not possible to imitate truly a dull and garrulous discourser, without repeating the effects of dullness and garrulity'. He then cites those parts of 'The Thorn' for approval 'which might as well or still better have proceeded from the poet's own imagination, and have been spoken in his own character'. There follow strictures on those parts which 'are felt by many unprejudiced and unsophisticated hearts, as sudden and unpleasant sinkings from the height to which the poet had previously lifted them, and to which he again re-elevates both himself and his reader'. (*Biographia Literaria.*) The section Coleridge mainly objects to is practically the whole of what might be regarded as the poem's second movement, stanzas 8–15, where the narrator gives the story which explains the woman's presence on the mountain-top. It is a section Wordsworth altered considerably after 1805, most of the alterations, according to Sélincourt, 'unfortunate even if more conventionally poetic'. (II, 513.) The question raised is one which concerns the whole poem and Wordsworth's tactical conduct of it: the whole poem rather than the two disparate parts either the cavilling Coleridge or the rationalizing Wordsworth would break it into, the one part a psychological study of a superstitious bore, the other the incommunicable conference of the mad woman in her solitude with the three things.

It is clear that the poem is not over by stanza 7. If it were finished here even those seven stanzas would not have the meaning that accrues to them once we have read on to the end and can return to them again (Wordsworth's beginning of 'The Thorn', like that of 'The White Doe', is also the end).

After stanza 7 there is an abrupt break. (Wordsworth uses a similar technique in 'Simon Lee'.) An impatient interlocutor demands to know the why's and wherefor's of all the mystery. His very repetition of the narrator's last words serves as link and as break with what has gone before. Thorn, pond, tree, and woman—they are reduced by his interruption to the level of a puzzle for which there must be some normal explanation. The numinous is utterly dispelled, as it requires to be, one might add, to prevent it from remaining the merely vague or from becoming the merely pretentious. We enter at a step (sinking from the height to which the poet had previously lifted us) the sphere of the commonplace and merely human:

> And they had fix'd the wedding-day,
> The morning that must wed them both;
> But Stephen to another maid
> Had sworn another oath;
> And with this other maid to church
> Unthinking Stephen went—
> Poor Martha! on that woful day
> A cruel, cruel fire, they say,
> Into her bones was sent:
> It dried her body like a cinder,
> And almost turn'd her brain to tinder.
>
> They say, full six months after this,
> While yet the summer-leaves were green,

She to the mountain-top would go,
And there was often seen,
'Tis said a child was in her womb,
As now to any eye was plain;
She was with child, and she was mad,
Yet often she was sober sad
From her exceeding pain.
Oh me! ten thousand times I'd rather
That he had died, that cruel father!

Sad case for such a brain to hold
Communion with a stirring child!
Sad case, as you may think, for one
Who had a brain so wild!
Last Christmas when we talked of this,
Old Farmer Simpson did maintain,
That in her womb the infant wrought
About its mother's heart, and brought
Her senses back again:
And when at last her time drew near,
Her looks were calm, her senses clear.

Effects of some subtlety are gained by Wordsworth's use of his retired sea-captain's mask:

But Stephen to another maid
Had sworn another oath—

this is to use repetition now for the effect of dry wit. The literary counter-point seals off the human enormity involved. The tragic circumstance is inevitably obvious, and so usual as to be thought of as also casual. The jaunty rhythm carries the sense both of Stephen's near-automatic unfaithfulness and the bystander's acceptance of it as only too much to be expected. The mood and recurrent human mode are compressible into the literary figure and the two short lines. The shallowness and the insentience of Stephen are there, as well as the ironic neighbour's salty awareness:

And with this other maid to church
Unthinking Stephen went—

The comment on Stephen's behaviour is not condemnatory. And the ambiguous adjective suggests again both his bucolic sleep-walking obliviousness of harmful intent, and his dangerous unawareness of the consequences that will flow from his action. The sharp result of this we get immediately. The lines are differently felt, though the same voice carries them to us:

> A cruel, cruel fire, they say,
> Into her bones was sent:
> It dried her body like a cinder,
> And almost turn'd her brain to tinder.

The narrator (a frequent habit) takes refuge in hearsay, but the imagery while challengingly prosaic is also apposite. The organic has been swept by fire and reduced to the inorganic. And this, we are made to understand, is what excess of experience can do to people, as we have already (from the first verse) become aware it can do to Thorn trees.

The withdrawal of the narrator behind the community is a significant resort of his, or device of Wordsworth's. He hides again behind 'old Farmer Simpson' who gave out as his opinion that after the ante-natal fever, the mother became quite sane again. Nor does the narrator know, nor anyone in the community, whether the child was born alive or dead. And though Martha 'about this time' would go up to the mountain-top, and though all that winter cries and voices were heard there, the captain, clinging to the factual, can only withdraw his assent from the common report:

> I cannot think whate'er they say,
> They had to do with Martha Ray.

We are left with the events and the facts and the rumours and with our own assessments. Wordsworth's use here of the narrator, both in his direct statement and in his evasions— Wordsworth's own disappearance behind the speaker and the speaker's indirectness—is cunningly calculated. We are on a similar footing with the poet, the captain, the captain's village, and the human facts.

It is at this point that the narrator gives his own first-hand report on Martha Ray, and we are taken back to the beginning of the poem, except that now there is the increment of meaning which comes from all that has intervened:

> 'Twas mist and rain, and storm and rain,
> No screen, no fence could I discover,
> And then the wind! in faith, it was
> A wind full ten times over.
> I looked around, I thought I saw
> A jutting crag, and off I ran,
> Head-foremost, through the driving rain,
> The shelter of the crag to gain,
> And, as I am a man,
> Instead of jutting crag, I found
> A woman seated on the ground.
>
> I did not speak—I saw her face,
> Her face it was enough for me;
> I turned about and heard her cry,
> 'O misery! O misery!'
> And there she sits, until the moon
> Through half the clear blue sky will go,
> And when the little breezes make
> The waters of the pond to shake,
> As all the country know,
> She shudders and you hear her cry,
> 'Oh misery! Oh misery!'

This fresh repetition places the central figure in a new light. But it is not the novelty that is important, and repetition is the wrong word. What Wordsworth says in his note on the poem concerning single phrases applies also to plot-items in the pattern of the narrative: it is a great error to imagine that the same incidents cannot be repeated without tautology. Tautology is what 'The Thorn' miraculously avoids. Imaginative insight into the meaning of the poem progressively deepens. We have had, for example, in the opening stanzas the setting of Thorn, pond, and hillock. Then followed the introduction into this setting of the woman. Her story took us a great way from this exposed *perdu* of the human situation—into the common village story of courtship, premarital betrayal, and abandonment: with madness starting up among the most familiar conditions. Then there was the hearsay of the village—callousness, incomprehension, magisterial condemnation, and superstition: from all of which the narrator was careful to detach himself. Now comes this episode of the narrator's direct encounter with both the Woman and the scene on the mountain, the raw impact of the shocking facts in their combined force. Stock reactions one after another have been tentatively indicated, only to be re-submitted to the test of the reality they would embroider or evade. And after the test they are dismissed. We come a second time upon the situation with which the poem begins in order that now we might see it after our minds have been scoured of irrelevancy, of the fanciful, the idly curious, the indolently compassionate, or the 'literary'. Thorn, pond, and hillock, and exposure on the mountain-top—these are now clearly related to the human situation, seen in terms of the crazed mother. Their meaning is amplified in that she now takes her place among them crouched 'like a jutting crag'. They are the emblems as well as the agents of a human plight—or a plight, rather, that includes the human but is metaphysically more extensive.

It is at this point Wordsworth makes his interlocutor insist on the final questions:

> 'But what's the thorn? and what's the pond?
> And what the hill of moss to her?
> And what's the creeping breeze that comes
> The little pond to stir?'

The questions are not answered. The narrator again draws

back from positive interpretation. Again he invokes the village commentators:

> I cannot tell; but some will say
> She hanged her baby on the tree,
> Some say she drowned it in the pond,
> Which is a little step beyond,
> But all and each agree,
> The little babe was buried there,
> Beneath that hill of moss so fair.

The muddy pond becomes a mirror in which the village sees its own poisonous fancy:

> Some say, if to the pond you go,
> And fix on it a steady view,
> The shadow of a babe you trace,
> A baby and a baby's face,
> And that it looks at you;
> Whene'er you look on it, 'tis plain
> The baby looks at you again.

But even the folk-fancy is a form of evasion. The babe, drowned or undrowned, is a psychic reality, a mystery centred in the woman and the Thorn: life either still-born, or blighted at its birth, a 'babe' lying like a death-giving hand on the heart of Martha. Swinburne was right to record 'the dreadfulness of a shocking reality' in his response to the poem, 'an effect of unmodified and haunting horror'.

The Babe's introduction at this point is a potent reminder of its appearance (almost as a passing irrelevance, an hallucination, or literary accident) at the beginning:

> There is a thorn; it looks so old,
> In truth you'd find it hard to say,
> How it could ever have been young,
> It looks so old and grey.
> Not higher than a two-years' child,
> It stands erect this aged thorn.

The woman and the Thorn at the end are both seen under

the shadow of that quelled or unrealized existence which the Babe stands for. Martha has already been associated closely with the 'pond', the breeze from heaven ruffling and distorting its surface, and the woman shuddering with each impact. Her last association with the thorn brings about Wordsworth's final development of his theme. The factual aspects of Martha's story (the police court interest in what happened exactly, and how) are relegated to their right place as mere accidents. Wordsworth's eye travels back from the woman to the three things and the mountain-top. Man's inhumanity to man is part of a larger context of anti-vital and elemental forces. There is in the poem the possibility of a betrayed mother murdering her child (a 'natural' action)—the possibility of a willed negation of life in view of life's destiny (the Thorn) and its conditions (the biting wind). But what we are left with is something more difficult, and harder to define. Life is not admitted as acceptable, nor is the denial of life willed: what we have is madness, something in whatever space there is between murder and suicide, madness brought on by a hurt beyond endurance that the victim is unwilling any other creature should share: a deadlock of anguish and compassion. Wordsworth's nephew worried about his uncle's early tendencies towards the twin errors of Stoicism and Pelagianism. 'The Thorn' shows such a worry to have been seriously misplaced: neither stoicism nor pelagianism are as open to anguish or as conscious of the mysterious horror in things as Martha. But a strong positive feeling accompanies the negatives at the end. Wordsworth's poem is the puerperal fever of one in the throes of compassion: it is the compassion that survives:

> I cannot tell how this may be,
> But plain it is, the thorn is bound
> With heavy tufts of moss, that strive
> To drag it to the ground.
> And this I know, full many a time,
> When she was on the mountain high,

71

By day, and in the silent night,
When all the stars shone clear and bright,
That I have heard her cry,
'O misery! O misery!
O woe is me! oh misery!'

III

GOSLAR POEMS

THE THORN and 'The Idiot Boy' are one way of maintaining balance among attitudes disruptive of the personality at its base: compassion that can neither with decency be suppressed nor move with any hope of effectiveness to alter the situation that has called it into being. Their achievement is what I have called the irony of loving-kindness. Pity is retained in its living warmth, yet the mind takes full note of the unalterables. The unalterables can too easily be wished away. Alternatively, it would be just as easy to recoil from them into despair. Since they cannot be removed they must be accepted. The Wordsworthian irony is not a means of evasion. The chasm between compassion and its object, as between the human and the natural, is neither wishfully bridged nor made into a joking incongruity. We are left at one extreme (of integration or alienation) with the Mad Mother and the Idiot, and, at the other, with *l'homme moyen sensuel* who is telling the stories: the simple-sane non-omniscient story-teller, a product of the average soil, a man surrounded by a more extensive world than his consciousness includes, and who thereby forces the reader of his story both to take in his story's full span and to reckon also with the story-teller's perdurable ordinariness and faulty comprehension. Of all things, however, compassion once awake is the least appeasable and the least repressible. It cannot persist unchanged in indefinite detachment. It must engage in order to share or in order to redeem. Driven from compassion one can only hope to hold on to patience. The basic human conditions cannot really be changed. Man can only calculate therefore what (for however large or small an order) there is to suppress or to re-view. In 'The Thorn' the old and the two-year-olds are seen frozen together in the single image of the gnarled tree. The tree itself is dragged down into, rather than assimilated to, or reconciled with, the mossy earth. In 'The Idiot Boy' the idiocy of old age separates off from the primal idiocy of Johnny, and both are held in suspension against a nature that is green and growing, though the process is inaudible to human ears deafened with the clamour of merely human needs. 'The Thorn' coming after 'The Idiot Boy', is a Wordsworthian nadir. Swinburne was maybe right to react to the essential horror of it.

Wordsworth already by this period had fully realized in poetry scenes of desolation, of human sequestration, of social harmony rendered impossible by the human conditions themselves. In the story of Margaret (*Excursion*, Bk. I, ll. 511 *seq*.) the family is torn apart, the human order is insupportable in its setting, the home disintegrates, house and garden are over-run, the drinking-place is moss-grown and disused:

> It was a plot
> Of garden ground run wild, its matted weeds
> Marked with the steps of those, whom, as they passed
> The gooseberry trees that shot in long, lank, slips,
> Or currants, hanging from their leafless stems,
> In scanty strings, had tempted to o'erleap
> The broken wall . . .
>   . . . Beside yon spring I stood,
> And eyed its waters till we seemed to feel
> One sadness, they and I. For them a bond
> Of brotherhood is broken: time has been
> When, every day, the touch of human hand

74

Dislodged the natural sleep that binds them up
In mortal stillness; and they ministered
To human comfort. Stooping down to drink,
Upon the slimy foot-stone I espied
The useless fragment of a wooden bowl,
Green with the moss of years, and subject only
To the soft handling of the elements:
There let it lie.

(Excursion, Bk. I, ll. 453–495)

This is an emotion vividly concrete, powerful, simple, and
end-stopped. The quietus is accepted, almost reposed in.
Wordsworth, however, had complex feelings, and above all,
a restlessness that could not quiet itself by simple collapse.
The only philosophy he knew was the eighteenth-century
one. And that was optimistic. It admitted the fact of fear
and the fact of hope, it took in pain as well as pleasure, but
it asserted that the final balance—for the mind and for the
universe—was one which left joy uppermost. The eighteenth century as it grew old found its raw compassion less
and less reconcilable with either a general eudaemonism or a
personal eupepsia. Wordsworth, by nature eupeptic, inheri-
ted both the torn conscience and the serene theory of the
eighteenth century, a theory that catered better for com-
placence than for anxious concern. 'The Thorn' and 'The
Idiot Boy' show him achieving balance among conflicting
feelings in one way, a way personal to himself. At the same
period, however, he was attempting to handle his compassion
and its objects in the traditional eighteenth-century mode,
the mode of the conceptualist rather than the intuitionist.
'The Old Cumberland Beggar' is the result: a poem curious
in that it was excluded from *Lyrical Ballads* (1798) and all
the more curious in the alleged 'fragment' from it which was
in fact incorporated in that volume: 'Old Man Travelling';
Animal Tranquillity and Decay'.

At first sight 'The Old Cumberland Beggar' looks very
much as if it were arguing for the worst form of reactionary

quietism and the most vapid form of eighteenth-century optimism—that which Blake bitingly reduced to its own self-condemnatory definition in the paradoxes of 'The Human Abstract':

> Pity would be no more
> If we did not make somebody poor;
> And Mercy no more could be
> If all were as happy as we.

Actually, Wordsworth does not fall into the traps set for fanatics of self-regarding benevolence. Two attitudes to the Beggar are possible. One is that of the politicians Wordsworth addresses in the poem. The other is that of the country folk he knows. The politician sees beggary as a social nuisance for which institutional provision will have to be made, as provision also has to be made for sewage-disposal or the collection of dust-bins. The country-folk continue to see the Beggar as a person, not a target for heartless hygiene but a constituent part of their human community. The Beggar is still within the circumambience of living sympathy. In fact he touches off in the countryman some of his deepest impulses, tenderness and respect for the individual. Wordsworth's thought is not original but neither is it trivial. Furthermore, as Wordsworth handles his theme, he certainly avoids the sweetness of soul that stinks. 'The Old Cumberland Beggar', however, is mainly important not for itself so much as for the lines 'Animal Tranquillity and Decay'. The close connection of the two poems is obvious. That the *Lyrical Ballads* (1798) passage is a rejected or excerpted passage from the longer poem, at some stage of its existence, would seem to be more doubtful. In the smaller poem we do not encounter merely some exercise or other of an eighteenth century ruminant. We have instead Wordsworth's immediate self-confrontation with an aspect of things not capable of accommodation to any system emphasizing 'comprehensiveness' of mind as the essential condition for integration, or any view of vital 'joy' as the only unifying emotion. One of the most striking things about the poem is its title—the association of tranquillity, animal being, and organic decay: a curious polar opposite to the trance experience of 'Tintern Abbey', and equally curious, perhaps, in the puzzle it proposes to any Wordsworthianism which takes its creed exclusively from that poem:

> The little hedgerow birds,
> That peck along the road, regard him not.
> He travels on, and in his face, his step,
> His gait, is one expression: every limb,
> His look and bending figure, all bespeak
> A man who does not move with pain, but moves
> With thought. He is insensibly subdued
> To settled quiet: he is one by whom
> All effort seems forgotten: one to whom
> Long patience hath such mild composure given,
> That patience now doth seem a thing of which
> He hath no need. He is by nature led
> To peace so perfect that the young behold
> With envy, what the Old Man hardly feels.

The old man, without effort and without consciousness, has what the young man can restlessly strive for, miss, and finally envy. At the end of *Prelude*, Bk. IV there is another such abrupt juxtaposition. Young Wordsworth, ecstatically re-unified once more after his first year at Cambridge, comes upon a figure in the moonlight that looks at first like a corpse. The corpse, however, turns out to be such another as this beggar-man: an old soldier unified about another centre, equally with the beggar beyond the accidents of experience by having endured past the point at which experience has any further power to give or to take away. The soldier speaks as one

> Remembering the importance of his theme
> But feeling it no longer.
>
> *Prelude*, Bk. IV, ll. 477–8)

The moment is important for Wordsworth. A question is put to the eighteenth-century 'grand principle of pleasure', and to his own willed faith in the happy wedlock of the mind and 'things'. There is a patience beyond patience, and which is not death. Wordsworth puts the antithesis of the usual Wordsworthian thesis with a compelling force and objectivity. There is no theory interposed between him and the new, strange fact. The animal, in decay, and far removed from 'animal delight', achieves the tranquillity every young animal could rightly wish his own. The Old Beggar and the Old Soldier go with the Mad Mother and the Idiot Boy. All have immunity and singleness. The Beggar and the Soldier, however, fall within the range of the organically normal. Both are 'by nature led to peace'. It is the immunity which constitutes the particular burden of the mystery of all this unintelligible world: immunity to pain, and resistance to rationalization. The Beggar becomes something more than a social problem. Even pity is irrelevant, at best something only redounding (in a non-eighteenth-century sense, now) to the advantage of those who bestow the alms. The Beggar is larger than life. He contains his secret in inscrutable dignity. If 'Animal Tranquillity and Decay' is a fragment of 'The Old Cumberland Beggar' the fragment is larger than the whole of which it is a part. It is insight raised to a higher power.

Wordsworth at this period is surprisingly various in his poetic methods, and in the genuinely different directions his explorations take. After *Lyrical Ballads* (1798) he went to Germany (September 1798–February 1799). There he wrote what have since been called his Goslar poems. The passage in *Prelude*, Bk. IV on the old Soldier belongs to the period of 'Animal Tranquillity and Decay' (1797). Goslar produces those parts of the *Prelude* concerning the Stolen Boat (I, 327–427), Skating (I, 452–89), the Boy who listened to the Owls (V, 389 *seq.*), and 'Nutting'. All deal with organically shaping experiences that have occurred in Wordsworth's

78

boyhood. They are diametrically opposed to the poems on the peace of age, and patience long-past-suffering. Then there are the *Lucy* poems and the *Matthew* poems. The latter are of especial importance in tracking Wordsworth down into the hiding places of his power at this time. For in both Wordsworth (experimentally maybe) brings together the young boy and the Old Man, animal delight and animal decay, the moment of the rose and the moment of the yew. The conversations are exploratory of the attitudes appropriate to both boyhood and old age, and to the placing of both in their mutual relation. The view of life must take in also the prospect of death.

'The Fountain' rings with the vital Wordsworthian confidence that age and childhood are still open to communicate with each other:

> We talked with open heart, and tongue
> Affectionate and true,
> A pair of friends, though I was young,
> And Matthew seventy-two.
>
> We lay beneath a spreading oak,
> Beside a mossy seat;
> And from the turf a fountain broke,
> And gurgled at our feet.

The boy and the old man are paralleled in the fountain and the spreading oak. These become two separate, but related, principles. However, fountain and oak belong to their own order: the order of that nature which, in 'The Idiot Boy', has both perdurable ebullience, and unoppugnable stability, and which stands over against the order friably or deciduously human. The Boy speaks for the fountain:

> 'Now, Matthew!' said I, 'let us match
> This water's pleasant tune
> With some old border song, or catch
> That suits a summer's noon;

79

'Or of the church-clock and the chimes
Sing here beneath the shade,
That half-mad thing of witty rhymes
Which you last April made.'

But Matthew, in his response, disappoints the expectations
of both boy and reader. His eye has been tracing the whole
arch of man's allotted span, and seeing it against its background not of eternity but of natural activity and harmonious
establishedness:

'No check, no stay, this streamlet fears;
How merrily it goes!
'Twill murmur on a thousand years,
And flow as now it flows.

'And here on this delightful day,
I cannot choose but think
How oft, a vigorous man, I lay
Beside this fountain's brink.

'My eyes are dim with childish tears,
My heart is idly stirred,
For the same sound is in my ears
Which in those days I heard.

'Thus fares it still in our decay:
And yet the wiser mind
Mourns less for what age takes away
Than what it leaves behind.'

The last stanza is another of Wordsworth's strange surprises.
It has all the startle and flash of wit, the eighteenth-century
dissecting antithesis, yet it takes too deep a plunge into
sobering considerations to have the effect of wit. The stock
mood expected in the poem at this point would be an old
man's nostalgia for his youth, regret for former days, envy of
the past. What we have in fact is something quite different:
a highly complex sorrow. The normal expectations are of

course satisfied: the transitoriness of life is suggested, the inevitability of declining powers, the involuntary tears (ambiguously called 'childish'—as if childhood were only a doubtful guide for the grown man's responses). But then comes the Wordsworthian turn. Age takes things away, but the worst is what age leaves behind, leaves, that is, as a kind of deposit in the personality. The movement away from childhood, through maturity, to old age is not a thing necessarily regrettable. In the last phase there should be an increment of 'gifts reserved for age'. But unfortunately this is not so. Age does not bring rest, or fulfilment, or cessation. Age therefore can neither want its boyhood or earlier manhood back, nor be content within itself. In wisdom one can neither wish the journey to stop short of its end, nor wish to repeat it, nor take satisfaction in the end achieved. Matthew points out the contrast in this respect ('The Idiot Boy' contrast) between animals and men:

> 'The Blackbird in the summer trees,
> The Lark upon the hill,
> Let loose their carols when they please,
> Are quiet when they will.
>
> 'With Nature never do *they* wage
> A foolish strife; they see
> A happy youth, and their old age
> Is beautiful and free:
>
> But we are pressed by heavy laws;
> And often, glad no more,
> We wear a face of joy, because
> We have been glad before.'

The main thing taken away by Age is 'household hearts that were his own'. The chief thing left is loneliness and the frustration of still active capacities for affection and joy. Wordsworth sees that the precariousness of joy consists in more than the mere failure of individual powers. It has to do

81

with the inevitable dissolution of the very group within which the individual's love is fostered and fed. The Boy volunteers to take the place of Matthew's family:

'Now both himself and me he wrongs,
The man who thus complains!
I live and sing my idle songs
Upon these happy plains,

'And, Matthew, for thy Children dead
I'll be a son to thee!'
At this he grasped his hands, and said,
'Alas! that cannot be.'

The *Matthew* poems are taut compressions of a fundamentally gnomic wisdom. They are lean and laconic. Their explosive force comes from their elliptical handling of incident. Meaning sparks across the deliberate gap or calculated change of attention. Such a gap occurs immediately after Matthew has replied to the Boy. The poem continues and ends with two verses as follows:

We rose up from the fountain-side:
And down the smooth descent
Of the green sheep-track did we glide,
And through the wood we went;

And, ere we came to Leonard's Rock,
He sang those witty rhymes
About the crazy old church clock
And the bewildered chimes.

Is this Matthew discovering again a genuine joy, or rehearsing again an old one, or is it the old man indulging a boy's fancy? Is the 'man of mirth' lending his voice to a blitheness as 'childish' as the tears he shed by the fountain and which can only exist in the willed dissociation that produces 'a half-mad thing of witty rhymes', half madness and half wit, something maybe similar in effect to Wordsworth's own

82

apparently dissociated quatrains, their springy gaiety of movement jarring grotesquely with the sombre overtones?

Shortly after the death of his brother John (in 1805) Wordsworth wrote:

> I have submitted to a new control:
> A power is gone which nothing can restore;
> A deep distress hath humanised my soul.
>
> (IV, p. 259)

Wordsworth is describing how, before that event, he had painted verbal pictures, of life and of nature, interpreting existence in terms of 'steadfast peace that might not be betrayed'. Actually, Wordsworth had submitted to a control deeper and eerier than anything that could naïvely be called either bliss or tranquillity long before 1805. The poems of the Goslar period themselves emanate from such a different centre. The poems recalling his childhood, the *Lucy* poems, the *Matthew* poems, are none of them 'happy'. The *Lucy* poems precede the *Matthew* poems in the German holiday. With one exception they have been rated, I am certain, too high in comparison with the poems that followed them. I am equally certain their apparent concern with a dead and beloved girl is not Wordsworth's psychic burial of an incest-wish focused on Dorothy. Here is the finest and most imaginative of their moments:

> A Violet by a mossy stone
> Half hidden from the eye!
> —Fair as a star when only one
> Is shining in the sky.

Maybe a psychiatrist would say this was the integrated health of the mind finding its expression, rather than repressed incestuousness venting itself by displacement of imagery. Lucy is the Violet. Wordsworth gives us the violet's shy courage and its vulnerability at once, its unrhetorical assertion of life as it half emerges, half escapes, from behind the stone—yet its threatened existence too, as if it were in danger from the stone crushing it or entombing it (moss, for Wordsworth, throughout this period, has frequently had this association). Then there is the violet's shrinking from notice—not merely embarrassment, but a virginal intactness, an inwardness and singleness any contact, sympathetic as well as hostile, would imperil (so that the mossy stone is a couch and a shield as well as a threat). Last, Lucy is the Star, with a star's unchallengeable serenity, its regal uniqueness in beauty and its supreme value in uniqueness, its singleness overpoweringly sufficient in itself without the attendant hosts it will herald or has already seen depart (the Star is Hesper-Vesper of the double name, the first vision of the fullness of beauty and the last brooding view of it). Finally there is the suggestion not only of supreme preciousness but also of authority with claims on our admiration, set, furthermore, at a distance above and beyond too close approach. It is this Lucy who is 'in her grave'—an immortal girl it is foolish to think of as being banished, a girl not so much dead as transcendent. Love infantile, incestuous, adult, or divine seems to find itself and go beyond itself in the lines. The two metaphors in the single stanza, as can happen in poetry, are again greater than the poem they form part of.

But, on the whole, the *Lucy* poems are not as inclusive as the *Matthew* poems. They do not succeed so subtly in the bringing together of youth and age, the moment of the rose and the moment of the yew, the violet and the mossy stone. In both 'The Fountain' and 'The Two April Mornings' the old man mourns a dead and unreplaceable child. But, again, the attitudes are broader and deeper than sorrow or regret. They have to do with those prior or succeeding powers of the mind that can contain both without repressing either.

'The Two April Mornings' is the story of an old man and a boy setting out as the sun is rising. It tells how the old man is struck with the thought of a time thirty years before (such another morning) when he was going off on a similar expedition. He came, then, to the churchyard where his young daughter was buried:

> 'Nine summers had she scarcely seen,
> The pride of all the vale;
> And when she sang;—she would have been
> A very nightingale.
>
> 'Six feet in earth my Emma lay,
> And yet I loved her more,
> For so it seemed, than till that day
> I e'er had loved before.
>
> 'And turning from her grave, I met,
> Beside the churchyard yew,
> A blooming Girl, whose hair was wet
> With points of morning dew.
>
> 'A basket in her hand she bare,
> Her brow was smooth and white;
> To see a child so very fair,
> It was a pure delight!
>
> 'No fountain from its rocky cave
> E'er tripped with foot so free;
> She seemed as happy as a wave
> That dances on the sea.'

The vision of the Girl is that of a Lucy still alive. What do we expect from Wordsworth now? Again the verse immediately following upsets the stock situations:

> 'There came from me a cry of pain
> Which I could ill confine;
> I looked at her, and looked again:
> And did not wish her mine.'

As with the 'gratitude' at the end of 'Simon Lee', and the half-mad song at the end of 'The Fountain', so here Wordsworth leaves it to the reader's own sense of things to interpret the 'sigh of pain': the reader's sense as it has been enabled, made capable of directed guess, by the careful articulation of the poem up to this climax. Feelings as multitudinous and as unified as those in 'She dwelt among untrodden ways' are concentrated in the visionary Girl. She embodies beauty and vitality. Yet her dazzling light and life is that of a fountain springing from 'a rocky cave'. With her basket, her brow, her hair pointed and lit with dew, she is richly particularized. Yet she is also 'a wave that dances on the sea', a transient particular ready to merge eventually again into the un-individual vast. She seems a girl like the dead daughter would have been, yet she is an identity separate and distinct from Emma. She has the quality of *that*-ness to which Words-worth always gives his deepest and most spontaneous re-sponse. Such an expansion enables us to move to a position from which, retrospectively, our uneasiness over Matthew's reactions to the thought of his dead daughter by her grave-side might be explained. That Matthew should love his daughter more when she was dead than when she had been alive struck something of a false note. Self-indulgence as self-delusion might enter into the feeling, as when the 'love' we feel is made more important than the object we feel it for.

The girl beside the churchyard yew is a complex and com-pelling invitation. The tacit choice proposed is important. It involves how we accept or turn away from the experience of death. Matthew's 'I did not wish her mine' takes us through this significant and difficult turn. He is not looking for a substitute for his dead daughter; nor is he seeing in the beauty of the living a compensation for the withdrawn beauty of the dead. Ambiguously and richly, 'I did not wish her mine' (after 'the sigh of pain') recalls with fresh clarity of impact the thought and the fact of the girl who is dead. The original pain of the loss is brought back without any of the mutings which the passage of time has given it. The words might mean, 'I did not wish her mine, to undergo all the risk of loss again'. Or maybe Matthew did not wish her his because no person can take the place of another. These are both attitudes of shrinkage from experience. The opposite non-self-regarding attitudes, however, are also activated. Before the vision of the Girl blooming beside the yew Matthew is taken out of himself: he did not wish her *his*. The befuddledness of the graveside feeling is dispelled. He sees both the Girl and the Yew, life and death, the joy and the pain, in all their sharpness before him, as though Things now were standing in God's unchanging eye, but not merely (with Yeats's desperate adolescence of feeling) 'in all the vigour of their blood'.

The verses describing the visionary Girl are as fine as the finest in the Lucy poems. The vision resolves the dichotomy of the eternal and the transient, the general and the particular. (There is as much in Wordsworth's 'a wave that dances on the sea' as in the similar image Shakespeare applied to Perdita.) The special situation of private loss is transcended too. So is habituation to loss and the attendant falsifications of memory. The Girl under the Yew strips away the bedizening gloss of memory. She restores to full freshness the fact of surpassing beauty and the shadow of death in which beauty stands. The passage as a whole maintains a perpetual motion through the highest and deepest, and yet also the most common, of feelings.

Wordsworth does not leave the poem here with Matthew's 'sigh of pain'. He brings it back to the actual, almost to the casual. The poet himself has just happened, as it were, to remember this boyhood occasion when the old man was recalling this time before Wordsworth was born. And Matthew now stands before him as Matthew was then, a curiously authoritative and archetypal figure, particular and yet symbolic, a village schoolmaster and yet a kind of Druid Orpheus:

> Matthew is in his grave, yet now
> Methinks I see him stand,

As at that moment, with a bough
Of wilding in his hand.

The *Lucy* poems are fragments from the larger complex
embraced more adequately, and presented with greater com-
pleteness and detachment in 'The Fountain' and 'The Two
April Mornings'.

IV

WORDSWORTH AND
'NATURE'

I

Wordsworth as he has appeared so far has been the poet of Fortitude rather than Nature, and of perturbed compassion rather than joy. His concern has been with a wounded society and with the wound in himself as the representative of all men of good will. There is a division between the nature that unites energy and peace, impulse and law, and the other natures man finds in his individual self and in the society of which he forms a part. And even these latter two are riven asunder.

The most deeply felt poems up to now have been dedicated to endurance and to tenderness—an endurance that must continue past the ultimate thresholds: desertion, poverty, the certainty of loneliness, death. On the one side *Lyrical Ballads* is early Wordsworth. The book expresses the young man whose radical hopes were disappointed but whose compassion survived. On the other, they are premonitory of the old Wordsworth who was to endure beyond, survive, and elegize a whole generation of his friends, re-enacting in factual experience what he had written of in the Matthew poems. Yet again, *Lyrical Ballads* is intrusive—an experiment in a mode of dramatic self-projection Wordsworth will later neither develop fully nor even repeat. Yet further, they integrate some of Wordsworth's profoundest attitudes, without benefit of eighteenth-century Priestley or nineteenth-century priest. They offer a poetry that must be accepted or rejected in its own right, a poetry as major as anything Wordsworth can do.

At this period Wordsworth stands outside the convention of the couplet and is writing too early to come within the later conventions of the aesthetic. He is a man addressing men. His poems are not 'articulated' in the eighteenth-century manner, nor is every rift loaded with verbal ore. Instead we have humble accommodations to straight statement and to ballad literariness, both meeting in the figure of the simple narrator who has somehow got to tell his story in verse. And in addition there are those constant surprises of quick moral and psychological turn, the suppleness and steadiness of a strong and sensitive mind. Technically, Wordsworth's great innovation at this period is the 'lyrical ballad' itself, the form in which story-teller, story, and poet-manipulator are reciprocally and dynamically related. The lyrical ballad at its best is a symphonic structure. It is not uni-linear like the traditional ballad. It does not express a one-strand feeling like the usual lyric. Its subtle plotting (as in 'The Thorn') makes the central situation to be seen in various lights. At the same time the lyrical centrality and singleness is preserved. The repetitions intensify, the changing contexts extend, the meaning.

The lyrical ballad, however, is only one of Wordsworth's poetic forms during this period. At the same time he is developing a new type of blank verse, and going back into his past. The first public indication of this mode is 'Lines composed a few miles above Tintern Abbey', the last poem in the *Lyrical Ballads* volume and the first pointer towards *The Prelude*. For immediately after *Lyrical Ballads*—while he and Dorothy were at Goslar—Wordsworth seems to have written most of *The Prelude*, Boks. I–II, as well as several famous passages which he afterwards disposed in various places throughout the later books.

With Quiller-Couch, I think Wordsworth took his new blank-verse manner from Coleridge, the Coleridge of the 'Conversation pieces'. The opening of *The Prelude* also seems to have Coleridge's 'Frost at Midnight' in mind. 'Tintern Abbey', too, shows clear signs of the Coleridge-Wordsworth concert of these years.

Coleridge had taken over the blank verse of the larger eighteenth-century ruminants that preceded him, and altered it into something peculiarly his own. The wooden Miltonese, the confident dressing-up of approved public theory in approved poetic costume (already modulated by Cowper into something not so stagey or inflated) Coleridge made the responsive vehicle for a genuine self-communion. His verse moves like water over moss. The 'conversations' are internal dialogues. They are a mind making itself up in flux and re-flux, not an overbearing iteration of pre-rehearsed assertions. The reader overhears. The poem is the living plasm of a psychic process delicately controlled. Immediate psychic life is just what his fore-runners lacked: Akenside, for example, in spite of the words and phrases, and sometimes the governing notions, he might have bequeathed to both Coleridge and Wordsworth. Coleridge brought in new material too. The physical environment in which the thinking solitary is placed becomes a living partner in the thinking. It provides objective correlatives for the personal process. Internal and external prompt each other, modify each other, stand for each other, in a way that makes it difficult to speak of subject and object as divided opposites, where the object is symbolic and the symbol an effort to grasp its object more entirely:

> The frost performs its secret ministry
> Unhelped by any wind. The owlet's cry
> Comes loud, and hark again!—loud as before . . .

Therefore all seasons shall be sweet to thee,
Whether the summer clothe the general earth
With greenness, or the red-breast sit and sing
Betwixt the tufts of snow on the bare branch
Of mossy apple-tree, while the nigh thatch
Smokes in the sun-thaw; whether the eave-drops fall
Heard only in the trances of the blast,
Or if the secret ministry of frost
Shall hang them up in silent icicles,
Quietly shining to the quiet Moon.

Here frost (the shaping spirit), wind (the quickening and sustaining mover), and the Moon (the final contemplator and patroness of the transformations, the grace that accepts and raises them to a new perfection of stillness) are inner as well as outer, all the more the one because so pregnantly the other. The mind is not only pronounced to be but demonstrates it is in fact what Akenside affirmed:

so doth Nature's hand,
To certain attributes which matter claims,
Adapts the finer organs of the mind:
So the glad impulse of those kindred powers
(Of form, of colour's cheerful pomp, of sound
Melodious, or of motion aptly sped)
Detains the enlivened sense; till soon the soul
Feels the deep concord, and assents through all
Her functions.
(*The Pleasures of the Imagination*, 1757, Bk. I, ll. 153–161)

'Frost at Midnight' is Coleridge's masterpiece in what he would call co-adunation. 'Tintern Abbey' follows it as a Wordsworthian comment and companion-piece. Not only has Wordsworth taken hints for the movement of his blank verse from Coleridge, but the form of his poem too answers Coleridge's. 'Frost at Midnight' is Coleridge exemplifying 'continuity of consciousness', Coleridge taking up the past into the present for the future. It records a moment of self-inspection, self-unification, and self-direction. Starting from the immediate situation of the cottage at night, with young Hartley Coleridge sleeping nearby, Coleridge's mind is carried back to his own childhood and its forward-looking longings, its intimations, deprivations, and frustrations. The thought then returns through the present of the father to the future as the son will realize it. Instead of London Hartley will have the Lakes to form him in his early years; in place of the loneliness his father knew at Christ's Hospital there will be warm, liberating, and living companionship. The concluding 'therefore all seasons shall be sweet to thee' is at once a hope, a resolve, and a deduction.

'Tintern Abbey' takes its cue from 'Frost at Midnight'. Wordsworth too will write his chapter of integrative autobiography. The present recalls a not too remote past of five years before. That leads to a meditation on how the past lives in and still feeds the present. There follows a confident hope that the present will in its turn feed the future:

> And now with gleams of half-extinguished thought,
> With many recognitions dim and faint,
> And somewhat of a sad perplexity,
> The picture of the mind revives again:
> While here I stand, not only with the sense
> Of present pleasure, but with pleasing thoughts
> That in this moment there is life and food
> For future years.

Immediately then Wordsworth turns to consider the difference between himself now and himself as boy and young man. He has lost 'the aching joy' and the 'dizzy raptures', but—turning to the present again—'other gifts', he concludes, 'have followed'. There has been loss. There is also 'abundant recompense':

> For I have learned
> To look on nature, not as in the hour
> Of thoughtless youth; but hearing oftentimes
> The still, sad music of humanity,

> Not harsh, nor grating, though of ample power
> To chasten and subdue. And I have felt
> A presence that disturbs me with the joy
> Of elevated thoughts; a sense sublime
> Of something far more deeply interfused,
> Whose dwelling is the light of setting suns,
> And the round ocean, and the living air,
> And the blue sky, and in the mind of man:
> A motion and a spirit that impels
> All thinking things, all objects of all thought,
> And rolls through all things.

The experience incremental to the dizzy rapture is one that chastens and subdues; the still sad music of humanity falls across the private ecstasy. 'Tintern Abbey' accepts this transition as natural and inevitable. The answer it makes to Coleridge is that even granted Hartley will grow up in the Wordsworthian environment, and himself become what Wordsworth once was, even so the next stage of accommodation to the human condition will also have to be gone through. The ecstatic harmony is only a phase in a larger movement that passes on, in individual experience, to eventual loss, at best to lodgment in the memory. But the cycle is repeated too for each new life that is lucky enough. This brings Wordsworth (again following the pattern of Coleridge's poem) to rest his eye on Dorothy. The strength of the 'Frost at Midnight' pattern is sufficient to make Wordsworth represent Dorothy not as she in fact was (only a year and nine months younger than himself) but as a young girl. For the purposes of the poem Dorothy has before her the period of aching joy and dizzy rapture:

> thou, my dearest Friend,
> My dear, dear Friend . . . in thy voice I catch
> The language of my former heart, and read
> My former pleasures in the shooting lights
> Of thy wild eyes. Oh! yet a little while
> May I behold in thee what I was once,
> My dear, dear Sister!

Wordsworth even echoes the final address of Coleridge to young Hartley, with its culminating reference to the Moon:

> Therefore let the moon
> Shine on thee in thy solitary walk;
> And let the misty mountain winds be free
> To blow against thee: and, in after years,
> When these wild ecstasies shall be matured
> Into a sober pleasure; when thy mind
> Shall be a mansion for all lovely forms,
> Thy memory be as a dwelling-place
> For all sweet sounds and harmonies; oh! then,
> If solitude, or fear, or pain, or grief,
> Should be thy portion, with what healing thoughts
> Of tender joy wilt thou remember me,
> And these my exhortations! Nor, perchance—
> If I should be where I no more can hear
> Thy voice, nor catch from thy wild eyes these gleams
> Of past existence—wilt thou then forget
> That on the banks of this delightful stream
> We stood together.

Coleridge's poem describes one loop in time, Wordsworth's two. Wordsworth extends Coleridge's forward look still further: to a time when he himself might be dead and Dorothy (she is now more like his daughter than his sister) surviving him. Dorothy will then be able to look back to this present (which will then be her past) and gather from it such a chastened joy as Wordsworth now is harvesting from five years ago. The complex shuttling backwards and forwards in time ends at length in the poem's present, in Wordsworth's dedicated love for the sister reading over his shoulder:

> Nor wilt thou then forget
> That after many wanderings, many years
> Of absence, these steep woods and lofty cliffs,
> And this green pastoral landscape, were to me
> More dear, both for themselves and for thy sake!

A curious result comes from putting 'Tintern Abbey'

alongside 'Frost at Midnight': it is Coleridge's poem, rather than Wordsworth's, that is the utterance of a 'nature-poet' with an implicit faith in Nature. Coleridge had never had the mystical communion. Notwithstanding, his poem ends with an unhesitant assurance that Nature will look after Hartley. Wordsworth had had the most Nature could give, and the most, therefore, it could take away. He includes the record of the high experience in his poem but is aware of the inevitability of loss. There is 'the deep power of joy' but there is also the other term: 'solitude, or fear, or pain, or loss'. The most that can be secured is a 'sober pleasure'. This will stand between the contrary poles. In it will be resolved the moment of the rose and the moment of the yew. The pattern is a more inclusive one than Coleridge's, and a sobering one certainly. The 'dear Babe' of 'Frost at Midnight' was to grow up to be a tragic disappointment to the hopes vested in him. We cannot conceive the later Coleridge repeating the earlier poem with conviction. The last we hear of 'Tintern Abbey', on the other hand, is that Wordsworth read it to the Duke of Argyle, when Wordsworth was seventy-eight. The 'dear, dear Friend' of the poem was still with him —helpless and lunatic:

he read the introductory lines descriptive of the scenery in a low clear voice. But when he came to the thoughtful and reflective lines the tones deepened, and he poured them forth with a fervour and almost passion of delivery which was very striking and beautiful. I observed that Mrs. W. was deeply affected by the reading. The strong emphasis that he put on the words addressed personally to the person to whom the poem is addressed struck me as almost unnatural at the time—'My dear, *dear* friend' ran the words,—'in thy wild eyes.' It was not till after the reading was over that we found out that the old paralytic and *doited* woman we had seen in the morning was the sister to whom T.A. was addressed, and her condition accounted for the fervour with which the old poet read lines which reminded him of their better days. But it was melancholy to think that the vacant silly stare which we had seen in the morning was from the 'wild eyes' of 1798.

(II, p. 517)

There could be no better evidence for the poet of 'Tintern Abbey' and the poet of 'The Thorn' being the same person. And Wordsworth at seventy-eight still had common ground with the Wordsworth of twenty-eight.

II

Apart from 'Tintern Abbey', *Lyrical Ballads* does not contain much, then, that could qualify Wordsworth for the title of 'nature-poet'. 'Frost at Midnight' touched a trigger in Wordsworth's mind. What it did not do, immediately, was make Wordsworth utilize the external scene as Coleridge habitually did. The itemizing of the landscape detail at the beginning of 'Tintern Abbey' is strangely inert. The plots of cottage-ground, with their hedgerows—

> hardly hedge-rows, little lines
> Of sportive wood run wild

—the orchard-tufts and wreaths of smoke, are scarcely central to the mood and matter of the poem, scarcely in fact relevant. The smoke indeed leads to a major irrelevance: the jejune and idle association of

> some Hermit's cave, where by his fire
> The Hermit sits alone.

To see Wordsworth as a 'nature-poet' properly in his place we might consider the modes of 'nature-writing' already practised, the types of writing Wordsworth was transcending.

A rough scale of 'nature-poetry' can be constructed. The first level is that of 'nature-notes', the counting of the streaks of the tulip, observations like 'black as the ash-buds in the front of March' or like 'willows *whiten*, aspens quiver'. Tennyson is a notorious repository of such detachable and detailed accuracies, Wordsworth—surprisingly—less so. His characteristic poetry is not predominantly visual. There is little in his work that would have elicited a communication from Gilbert White. Few Wordsworth passages are comparable with the following from Coleridge's 'This Lime-Tree Bower My Prison' (of June 1797):

> The roaring dell, o'erwooded, narrow, deep,
> And only speckled by the mid-day sun;
> Where its slim trunk the ash from rock to rock
> Flings arching like a bridge;—that branchless ash,
> Unsunn'd and damp, whose few poor yellow leaves
> Ne'er tremble in the gale, yet tremble still
> Fann'd by the water-fall! and there my friends
> Behold the dark green file of long dank weeds,
> That all at once (a most fantastic sight!)
> Still nod and drip beneath the dripping edge
> Of the blue clay-stone.

This is the kind of attention to detail that Dorothy had and Wordsworth can be imagined as relying on her to supply. Wordsworth was not pre-eminently a note-taker in front of objects. If he ever had been his mature habit was to suppress or ignore the visual. He deplores the time when he was in that state

> In which the eye was master of the heart
>
> (*Prelude*, Bk. XI, ll. 105–20)

The eye as such is

> in every stage of life
> The most despotic of our senses.
>
> (*Prelude*, Bk. XI, ll. 171–4)

The second level is that at which the observer sees not only single details but is interested in drawing the whole scene. The words *draw* and *scene* are significant here. 'Scenery' was invented for the theatre before it was discovered in the world at large. 'Draw' indicates the nearness of the poet to the painter in the act of composition. The eighteenth century abounds in nature-poetry of this sort. It is, among other things, the century of the picturesque. Poets painted their scenes as painters composed their pictures. Even the standard browns and varnished yellows overflow from the easel on to the page of print: in Akenside, for example (he supplied 'Tintern Abbey' with its phrase 'the guide, the guardian')[1] with whom Wordsworth comparisons are sometimes made:

> I looked and lo! the former scene was changed;
> For verdant valleys and surrounding trees,
> A solitary prospect, wide and wild,
> Rushed on my senses. 'Twas a horrid pile
> Of hills with many a shaggy forest mixed,
> With many a sable cliff and glittering stream.
> Aloft, recumbent o'er the hanging ridge,
> The brown woods waved; while over-trickling springs
> Washed from the naked roots of oak and pine
> The crumbling soil; and still at every fall
> Down the steep windings of the channelled rock,
> Remurmuring, rushed the congregated floods
> With hoarser inundation; till at last
> They reached a grassy plain, which from the skirts
> Of that high desert spread her verdant lap,
> And drank the gushing moisture, where confined
> In one smooth current, o'er the lilied vale
> Clearer than glass it flowed. Autumnal spoils
> Luxuriant, spreading to the rays of morn,
> Blushed o'er the cliffs whose half-encircling mound,
> As in a sylvan theatre, enclosed
> That flowery level. On the river's brink
> I spied a fair pavilion, which diffused
> Its floating umbrage 'mid the silver shade
> Of osiers. Now the western sun revealed,
> Between two parting cliffs, his golden orb,
> And poured across the shadow of the hills,
> On rocks and floods, a yellow stream of light
> That cheered the solemn scene. My listening powers
> Were awed, and every thought in silence hung.
> (*The Pleasures of the Imagination*, 1744. Bk. II, ll. 271–300)

This is the interest in 'scenery' of the old-fashioned Camera

[1] *The Pleasures of the Imagination*, 1744: Bk. I l. 22.

Club—an interest Wordsworth practically never gives way to in his poetry, or not for long.

At a third level we have to do with Ruskin's 'pathetic fallacy'. Now there is the whole scene, maybe closely observed, presented with due regard to composition, but in addition made the vehicle for feelings originating in the beholder. The result, vulgarly, is 'atmosphere'. Dickens is an obvious master of this manner (the second chapter of *Bleak House*), and so of course are Virginia Woolf and D. H. Lawrence; in poetry, among the romantics, Keats and Shelley, among the Victorians Tennyson especially. The opening of 'The Lotos Eaters' is a good instance of what was to become almost a model for 'poetic' description in the nineteenth century. There is nothing comparable with 'The Lotos Eaters' in Wordsworth. In the Tennyson passage the variations of pictorial image only emphasize the sameness and averageness of the supporting mood. Tennyson requires us to surrender to the hypnotic melancholy. Wordsworth insists on the opposite: that we should become awake and aware, adjusting our selves to things, not things to us.

This brings us to the fourth level of interest in 'nature'. The three so far indicated are possible in anyone of average capacities. The threshold between the third and the fourth levels, however, seems to be more than usually steep. And it is over this threshold that the peculiarly Wordsworthian is found. The difference is not so much between two different kinds of writing as between two radically different mental attitudes, or kinds of mind. The attitude beyond the threshold Wordsworth himself described as 'wise passiveness'.

Wordsworth's 'passiveness' is clearly not a condition of relaxation, or of what Keats will call 'indolence'. It assumes, rather, a strenuous discipline of mind. It is a condition of calm and attentiveness, a state of receptiveness that is also vividly alert. Wordsworth's favourite adjective for it is *wakeful.* He talks of a 'watchful heart still *couchant.* . . . And an eye practised like a blind man's touch'. *Couchant,* suggesting both 'lying down' and 'crouching heraldically ready to spring' stresses the activity that is an important component in the passiveness. One is active at these times as one is when one is listening well. The opposite condition Wordsworth would describe in terms of 'dizzy perturbation'. Passiveness includes the swirling activity of perturbation but escapes its confusedness.

Wordsworth had the first germ of the idea in March 1798. A jotting of that time refers to 'holy indolence A most wise passiveness'—anticipating Keats's word if not his meaning. In *Lyrical Ballads* 'The Tables Turned' and 'Expostulation and Reply' are the hearty propaganda of the attitude. Neither of these poems, however, attempts an adequate exemplification of what Wordsworth had in mind. What Wordsworth did have in mind is exemplified in the autobiographical blank verse. Fuller philosophical exposition is reserved for *The Prelude*—that twelve-book-long expansion of 'Tintern Abbey' and of the implications of 'Frost at Midnight'.

The expanded accounts (most of the relevant *Prelude* passages belong to the period just after *Lyrical Ballads*) begin with Wordsworth's intuition of how growth from child to man is possible. The recurrent symbol of the River appears. The River combines change and permanence, deflection and yet prevailing steadiness of direction. While he was still an infant the River 'sent a voice that flow'd along his dreams':

> For this, didst Thou
> O Derwent! travelling over the green Plains
> Near my 'sweet Birthplace', didst thou, beauteous Stream,
> Make ceaseless music through the night and day
> Which with its steady cadence, tempering
> Our human waywardness, compos'd my thoughts
> To more than infant softness, giving me,

Among the fretful dwellings of mankind,
A foretaste, a dim earnest, of the calm
That Nature breathes among the hills and groves.

(Prelude, Bk. I, ll. 276–85)

The basic Wordsworthian concern is with the transactions that take place between the living person and his environment. Nature comes into the account, in the first instance, as a subordinate thing—as a part only (albeit a large part) of the world in which life happens. The child's first responses are to the mother:

>   blest the Babe,
> Nurs'd in his Mother's arms, the Babe who sleeps
> Upon his Mother's breast, who, when his soul
> Claims manifest kindred with an earthly soul,
> Doth gather passion from his Mother's eye!
> Such feelings pass into his torpid life
> Like an awakening breeze, and hence his mind
> Even (in the first trial of its powers)
> Is prompt and watchful, eager to combine
> In one appearance, all the elements
> And parts of the same object, else detach'd
> And loth to coalesce. Thus, day by day,
> Subjected to the discipline of love,
> His organs and recipient faculties
> Are quicken'd, are more vigorous, his mind spreads,
> Tenacious of the forms which it receives.
> In one beloved presence, nay and more,
> In that most apprehensive habitude,
> And those sensations which had been deriv'd
> From this beloved Presence, there exists
> A virtue which irradiates and exalts
> All objects through all intercourse of sense.
> No outcast he, bewilder'd and depress'd;
> Along his infant veins are interfus'd
> The gravitation and the filial bond
> Of nature, that connect him with the world.
> Emphatically such a Being lives,
> An inmate of this *active* universe;

From nature largely he receives; nor so
Is satisfied, but largely gives again,
For feeling has to him imparted strength,
And powerful in all sentiments of grief,
Of exultation, fear, and joy, his mind,
Even as an agent of the one great mind,
Creates, creator and receiver both,
Working but in alliance with the works
Which it beholds.—Such, verily, is the first
Poetic spirit of our human life;
By uniform control of after years
In most abated or suppress'd, in some,
Through every change of growth or of decay,
Pre-eminent till death.

(Prelude, Bk. II, ll. 239–80)

Already Wordsworth has developed the notion that the child is father of the man, and that the genius is merely a child whose growth has not been at any stage arrested. Continuity of consciousness is a prime requisite. The mind unifies itself. The past must be kept alive in the present for the future. Wordsworth's is a *dynamic* Hartleyanism. Memory is an active function of mind, forward-moving rather than backward-looking:

Thus, often in those fits of vulgar joy
Which, through all seasons, on a child's pursuits
Are prompt attendants, 'mid that giddy bliss
Which, like a tempest, works along the blood
And is forgotten; even then I felt
Gleams like the flashing of a shield; the earth
And common face of Nature spake to me
Rememberable things; sometimes, 'tis true,
By chance collisions and quaint accidents
Like those ill-sorted unions, work suppos'd
Of evil-minded fairies, yet not vain
Nor profitless, if haply they impress'd
Collateral objects and appearances,
Albeit lifeless then, and doom'd to sleep

103

Until maturer seasons call them forth
To impregnate and to elevate the mind.

(Prelude, Bk. I, ll. 609–24)

These passages are the great outworkings of 'Tintern Abbey'. They are the adapted and modified optimism of the classic eighteenth century felt on the pulses. The mind is purposive and responsive memory: memory not inert or nostalgic but self-vivifying and self-regulative. *The Prelude* is the last intellectual deepening that the eighteenth-century tradition of Locke, Hartley, and Priestley will be capable of, the last assertion of a rooted joy that is not merely a self-congratulatory complacency. In its great moments of confrontation and re-call the present restores and re-animates the past. The master-light of all our seeing is the capacity to re-act. The secret of maturity is to connect. Two further *loci classici* for Wordsworth's central thought at this time might be cited from *The Prelude*. The first opens Book XII:

From nature doth emotion come, and moods
Of calmness equally are nature's gift,
This is her glory; these two attributes
Are sister horns that constitute her strength;
This two-fold influence is the sun and shower
Of all her bounties, both in origin
And end alike benignant. Hence it is,
That Genius which exists by interchange
Of peace and excitation, finds in her
His best and purest Friend, from her receives
That energy by which he seeks the truth,
Is rouz'd, aspires, grasps, struggles, wishes, craves,
From her that happy stillness of the mind
Which fits him to receive it, when unsought.

(Prelude, Bk. XII, ll. 1–14)

The second is the epiphany Wordsworth experienced on Snowdon, in a walking-tour of 1793:

I looked about, and lo!
The Moon stood naked in the Heavens, at height

Immense above my head, and on the shore
I found myself of a huge sea of mist,
Which, meek and silent, rested at my feet:
A hundred hills their dusky backs upheaved
All over this still Ocean, and beyond,
Far, far beyond, the vapours shot themselves,
In headlands, tongues, and promontory shapes,
Into the Sea, the real Sea, that seem'd
To dwindle, and give up its majesty,
Usurp'd upon as far as sight could reach.
Meanwhile, the Moon look'd down upon this shew
In single glory, and we stood, the mist
Touching our very feet; and from the shore
At distance not the third part of a mile
Was a blue chasm; a fracture in the vapour,
A deep and gloomy breathing-place through which
Mounted the roar of waters, torrents, streams
Innumerable, roaring with one voice.
The universal spectacle throughout
Was shaped for admiration and delight,
Grand in itself alone, but in that breach
Through which the homeless voice of waters rose,
That dark deep thoroughfare had Nature lodg'd
The Soul, the Imagination of the whole.
   A meditation rose in me that night
Upon the lonely Mountain when the scene
Had pass'd away, and it appear'd to me
The perfect image of a mighty Mind,
Of one that feeds upon infinity,
That is exalted by an underpresence,
The sense of God, or whatsoe'er is dim
Or vast in its own being, above all
One function of such mind had Nature there
Exhibited by putting forth, and that
With circumstance most awful and sublime,
That domination which she oftentimes
Exerts upon the outward face of things,
So moulds them, and endues, abstracts, combines,
Or by abrupt and unhabitual influence

Doth make one object so impress itself
Upon all others, and pervade them so
That even the grossest minds must see and hear
And cannot chuse but feel. The Power which these
Acknowledge when thus moved, which Nature thus
Thrusts forth upon the senses, is the express
Resemblance, in the fulness of its strength
Made visible, a genuine Counterpart
And Brother of the glorious faculty
Which higher minds bear with them as their own.
That is the very spirit in which they deal
With all the objects of the universe;
They from their native selves can send abroad
Like transformations, for themselves create
A like existence, and, whene'er it is
Created for them, catch it by an instinct;
Them the enduring and the transient both
Serve to exalt; they build up greatest things
From least suggestions, ever on the watch,
Willing to work and to be wrought upon.

(Prelude, Bk. XIII, ll. 40–100)

Here the resolution Wordsworth has been seeking is given explicit statement. The 'sister horns' of the altar to which the individual must cling, and from which he will draw his strength, 'the sun and the shower', are 'emotion' and 'calmness', 'peace and excitation'. And the contraries seek each other in interchange. The experience on Snowdon was an instance of unification happening outside the mind, yet an external activity answering the mind's own. In the 1805 version the sea (the underpresence) gives up its majesty to the cloaking mist (the phenomenal). Yet in the centre of the mist remains 'a fracture in the vapour'—a central nothingness umbilically connecting the finite given to the infinite giver, and

in that breach

Through which the homeless voice of waters rose,
That dark deep thoroughfare, had Nature lodg'd
The Soul, the Imagination of the whole.

Wordsworth avoided the dichotomy of realism and con-
ceptualism. He needed a theory that would represent the
universe as an *active* one, observable only through corres-
pondingly active observation on the part of the beholder.
The imagery of 'receiving and giving' is necessarily misleading. The opposed parts of the image look like opposed
philosophies. Wordsworth's aim, however, was to steer
through the Scylla and Charybdis. The activity he knew was
an activity that grasped and an activity that held open its
hands. The key word is *activity*. So Wordsworth dropped
'holy indolence' early, as weighting the matter too exces-
sively on one side. His phrase 'wise passiveness' is inflected
into sense through its adjective, though 'Expostulation and
Reply' is a reckless short-hand for what is in his mind during
the months of 1798.

One major peculiarity of Wordsworth's mind is connected
with this 'interchange' he so many times tries to explain, and
which so many times has been taken as his 'mysticism'. As
we have seen, 'passiveness' is not an adequate word for the
relation. What Wordsworth was trying to describe was
something almost organic. It had to do with the traffic between the inner and the outer. It was like assimilation, or like
translation. Again, maybe, following a hint from 'Frost at
Midnight' which he developed much further, Wordsworth
resorts to the analogue of dreams to suggest what happens in
his most wakeful moments. They are also moments like his
famous one of clutching at the gate to see that, after all, it
was a gate outside him—a not unusual experiment in
adolescence. Early in his life, however, Wordsworth had
memorably felt the peculiar coincidence of inner and outer:

> Nor seldom did I lift our cottage latch
> Far earlier, and before the vernal thrush
> Was audible, among the hills I sate
> Alone, upon some jutting eminence
> At the first hour of morning, when the Vale
> Lay quiet in an utter solitude.

How shall I trace the history, where seek
The origin of what I then have felt?
Oft in these moments such a holy calm
Did overspread my soul, that I forgot
That I had bodily eyes, and what I saw
Appear'd like something in myself, a dream,
A prospect in my mind.

(*Prelude*, Bk. II, ll. 359–371)

Eighteenth-century long poems were either regurgitations of predigested thought, exercises in visual contrivance, or judicious combinations of the two. We have already stressed Wordsworth's (mature) avoidance of the picturesque. The blank verse chain of post-Lockean or post-Shaftesbury concepts he also put away. His philosophical poetry is, as Coleridge said (Dr. Leavis was right to point out how small such a claim might be) the greatest since Milton. *The Prelude* would have been unlikely as a form if the tradition from Dryden to Cowper had not already been established. But Wordsworth's modification of the meditative-perambulatory manner is his own. Wordsworth's verse is genuinely ruminant. The raw experience (the 'excitation') and the thoughtful assimilation of it (the 'calm') are co-present. Both weigh equally in the total experience. The discipline of wise passiveness extends its control to Wordsworth's use of words. Wordsworth's theory of the mind as living memory puts little strain between him and language. For language itself acts like the Wordsworthian mind. Words are repositories of potential opportunities. They record, recall, resolve, prognosticate, prepare. The act of using them in their immediate uniqueness of context affords also the 'excitation' peculiar to composition. At the same time the act of composing itself aims at putting down something already found, for the sake of future reference. This is maybe a wildly metaphorical way of stating an elusive case. In alternative short-hand we might remark that—maybe of set purpose—there is little in Wordsworth of the 'concrete' image, and equally little of prose

definition of statement. The verse of Wordsworthian rumi-
nation spans between these, in the same way as what might
be called his 'memories' avoid being merely drifting icebergs
from his past.

A good example of the developed Wordsworthian vision
and of Wordsworth's achieved poetic manner is already dis-
coverable in *Lyrical Ballads*—the opening lines of 'Tintern
Abbey'. Whenever Wordsworth is at his best the natural
scene he stands before is assimilated to something other. It
ceases to be something merely external and becomes what
may be called a mental landscape, a state of being the mind
partakes of with the object and the object with the mind.
Father Witcut, in a Jungian examination of his verse, has
characterized Wordsworth as an introverted sensationist.
Certainly, Wordsworth ignores the extrovert view. He takes
things into himself in their 'thingness'. There is nothing of
Keats in his reactions. His most characteristic passages have,
therefore, a haunting inwardness:

> Five years have past; five summers, with the length
> Of five long winters! and again I hear
> These waters, rolling from their mountain springs
> With a soft inland murmur.—Once again
> Do I behold these steep and lofty cliffs,
> That on a wild secluded scene impress
> Thoughts of more deep seclusion; and connect
> The landscape with the quiet of the sky.

The inwardness is at once apparent. The enumeration of the
years in terms of their 'five summers, with the length of five
long winters' is sober and steadying. The alternation is that
of Wordsworth's own two natures, 'joy the one, the other
melancholy' (*Prelude*, Bk. X, 865–6), and the cycle of fulfilment, loss, return. There is no suggestion, it will be noticed,
of how the river looks. Instead we are given to ponder on
'these waters'. The generalizing words put the particular
Wye into the context of the originating biblical element.
Wordsworth is not interested in the immediate sights and

sounds, although in 'spring' and in 'soft murmur' we get something of the mingled sharpness and mutedness of river noises. The river is mainly apprehended, however, as massively *rolling*—'rolling from mountain springs'. The full impression is one not of a river momentarily seen or heard but of a river felt as a continuing entity. Its total career includes the mountain spring which is its source and the sea which is its destination. And it rolls rather than runs. The word has massive permanence and authority. Wordsworth, as Whitehead would say, apprehends the river as an event, in time and space, and in the continuum that embraces both. For besides the mountain spring Wordsworth has in mind the ultimate sea. It comes in (by way of negative exclusion) in the expressively Wordsworthian 'inland'. Wordsworth's 'inland' always works in this way:

> Hence in a season of calm weather,
>   Though *inland* far we be,
> Our souls have sight of that immortal sea
>   Which brought us hither.

or *The Prelude*'s

> more than *inland* peace
> Left by the sea wind passing overhead.
> (Prelude, II, BK. ll. 115–16)

More notably, Wordsworth sees the whole region of river and cliff, mountain origin and sea-estuary, and *connects* it 'with the quiet of the sky'. What Wordsworth is doing here is almost impossible to transcribe. The effect is cumulative and has to do with the total psychic landscape his poetry tends to build up: with the accrued meanings of 'river', 'sea', and 'sky' in his verse as words in a real 'language of nature' and as items in the inner language of the poet. To this aspect of his poetry generally we shall return later. Meanwhile, another excerpt from *The Prelude* illustrates a similar thing, and in language that lends itself more easily to analysis:

There was a Boy, ye knew him well, ye Cliffs
And Islands of Winander! many a time
At evening, when the stars had just begun
To move along the edges of the hills,
Rising or setting, would he stand alone
Beneath the trees, or by the glimmering Lake,
And there, with fingers interwoven, both hands
Press'd closely, palm to palm, and to his mouth
Uplifted, he, as through an instrument,
Blew mimic hootings to the silent owls
That they might answer him.—And they would shout
Across the watery Vale, and shout again,
Responsive to his call, with quivering peals,
And long halloos, and screams, and echoes loud
Redoubled and redoubled; concourse wild
Of mirth and jocund din! And when it chanced
That pauses of deep silence mock'd his skill,
Then sometimes, in that silence, while he hung
Listening, a gentle shock of mild surprize
Has carried far into his heart the voice
Of mountain torrents; or the visible scene
Would enter unawares into his mind
With all its solemn imagery, its rocks,
Its woods, and that uncertain Heaven, receiv'd
Into the bosom of the steady Lake.

(*Prelude*, Bk. V, ll. 389–413)

The passage italicized can bear particular scrutiny. What
begins as reminiscence ends as a curiously deepened psychological insight, and the verbal transmission of both. 'Then
sometimes' begins the series of re-distributions that the
whole passage affects. 'Then' means 'at that dramatic point
in time'; it carries a sense of the arbitrarily given and the
unanticipated. It can also mean 'at that stage in the process
of events, as an inevitable consequence of what had gone
before', i.e. the opposite of the merely arbitrary: 'a somewhat
will happen now only until it happens we cannot know what
it is'. The inevitable and the indeterminate balance in the
word as they do in all acts of real entry into experience.

III

'Sometimes' works in two complementary ways to 'then'. First, it is a surprising reminder that the experience was not unique, and that it did not happen every time the Boy hooted. This underlines that aspect of the event which was arbitrary. The word insists too, however, that the Boy's game with the owls was habitual, and that the special experience about to be described, while not mechanically inevitable, was in fact recurrent. In conjunction like this, therefore, 'then' and 'sometimes' counterpoint each other. If the first is taken in its causal sense this is immediately corrected by the casual which 'sometimes' brings in. If 'then' is taken as 'at that particular moment' the other comes back with its insistence of the repeated occasions the hooting was performed. The two words together, by their paradoxical oppositions, point to something ingrained in the nature of experience: something which, in their differing ways, Zeno and Heraclitus abstract from the stillness and the flux of actuality. Wordsworth gives us in the *now* of the reading a verbal experience managed in the same terms of living as are valid for all such moments.

The flux of the same kind of meanings that goes on in 'Then . . . sometimes' recurs throughout the passage. 'Hung . . . listening', for example: the utter helpless passivity of the one (the *dependence*) and the alert self-collectedness of the other; or the remarkable clashes and appropriatenesses of 'gentle . . . shock', or 'mild . . . surprise' (in the seventeenth century they would be noted as 'witty'). Here the disparates are again brought together. There is excitation and calm, tension and repose. The primary experience is actual biography for the poet. It is also given to the reader in words. Only as we allow the words to work to their due ends can we admit and as it were re-experience the piece of biography Wordsworth is relating.

A further effect is gained in the passage by what appears as a dis-arrangement of the logic of events. The sound of the mountain torrents was carried to the Boy through the silence, and its 'gentle shock' was then noticed with 'mild surprise'. Such would be the normal sequence. Wordsworth, however, typically, transposes subject and object in his sentence:

> a gentle shock of mild surprise
> Has carried far into his heart the voice
> Of mountain torrents.

The result is to suggest the simultaneousness of both factors in the unitary event. The heart opens more fully to the gentle shock of its own first awakening, to admit the voice more deeply; and in the consequently deepened apprehension the external voice of the torrents (Wordsworth's River again) becomes the internal voice of the heart. Heart and torrent are one. This exchange of inner and outer (parallelled by what happens in 'The Solitary Reaper', or in the 'inland murmur' of 'Tintern Abbey') prepares for the further development of this effect in the lines immediately following. (It may be noted again how the word 'unawares' is a transference back from the Boy to the scene: logically it is the Boy who is unaware, but syntactically it is the scene that is made to seem so):

> or the visible scene
> Would enter unawares into his mind
> With all its solemn imagery, its rocks,
> Its woods, and that uncertain heaven received
> Into the bosom of the steady Lake.

With these last two lines the benevolent circle is complete. The scene entering the Boy's mind is like 'the uncertain heaven' entering 'the bosom of the steady Lake'. Lake and mind are one. The Lake is the mind opening to and receiving what, in 'Tintern Abbey', is 'the quiet of the skies'. The Boy taking the scene into his bosom is the Lake. 'Uncertain heaven' takes us back to the kind of thing we have already examined in 'Then . . . sometimes'. This heaven is not uncertain in the sense that we are not sure that it exists, or of what it thinks about us, or whether it is right to call it 'heaven'. Rather, once again, the words marry exquisitely the flux and the stillness, time and eternity, the transient moment and the permanent possibility of recurrence.

III

Wordsworth at this period realizes in lived response what is implied in the dead metaphor 'the language of nature'. We might regard it as recurrent imagery merely. Or, on the other hand, we might see it as obsessional. Again, it could be dismissed as normal for one brought up in the particular environment of Cumberland, and returning to make his home there in his maturity, with a nostalgic hope and a prospect of self-recovery that were not disappointed. In any case, the language of the Cumberland landscape was one Wordsworth knew. He used it to discover himself and to express himself—the river, the lakes, the reflections in water, the woods, rocks, mountains, clouds, winds; birds, flowers, and the moon and stars. There is little in his poetry that is merely scenic. What Wordsworth does is to make the items of the eighteenth century picturesque speak. His landscape, cumulatively, develops a mind of its own that he responds to. The items enumerated are the main interlocutors. The river of his boyhood we have already mentioned. It flowed along his dreams in *The Prelude* (Bk. I, l. 276) and he rediscovered its significance in 'Tintern Abbey'. Who, he asks (*Prelude*, Bk. II, ll. 214) can portion the river of his mind? The brook forced into a channel (*Prelude*, Bk. IV, ll. 39–55) seemed once a satire on himself. Yet again (*Prelude*, Bk. IV, ll. 110–11) he 'sauntered like a river murmuring and talking to itself'. Dorothy, during his period of stress, accompanied him as a river runs by a road:

> then it was
> That the beloved Woman in whose sight
> Those days were pass'd, now speaking in a voice

Of sudden admonition, like a brook
That did but cross a lonely road, and now
Seen, heard, and felt, and caught at every turn,
Companion never lost through many a league,
Maintained for me a saving intercourse
With my true self.

(*Prelude*, Bk. X, ll. 908–16)

Wordsworth needs the river imagery again to describe what Dorothy did for him:

but for thee sweet Friend,
My soul, too reckless of mild grace, had been
Far longer what by Nature it was framed,
Longer retained its countenance severe,
A rock with torrents roaring, with the clouds
Familiar, and a favourite of the stars:
But thou didst plant its crevices with flowers,
Hung it with shrubs that twinkle in the breeze,
And teach the little birds to build their nests
And warble in its chambers.

(*Prelude*, Bk. XIII, ll. 226–36)

Even in the sonnet 'On Westminster Bridge' the culminating symbol of enduring peace and purposiveness is:

The river glideth at its own sweet will.

The landscape he knew provided Wordsworth with fluid meanings rather than with fixed symbols. His own sense for sameness and change was carried out in the words nature spoke with. Thus the river comes from the torrent, and the torrent breaks from the mountain, issues into the lake, and finds its way eventually to the sea. The sea, in the eighteenth-century language of the Sublime, combines both mountain and lake:

Two voices are there; one is of the sea,
One of the mountains . . .
. . . what sorrow would it be
That mountain floods should thunder as before,

And Ocean bellow from his rocky shore,
And neither awful Voice he heard by thee!

(III, p. 115)

The lake is the mirror of the receptive consciousness. With
it Wordsworth associates the pool, and reflection—the lake
at its most quiet, mirroring the quiet sky. Winds are like
rivers, only of air: as in Coleridge, prompting agencies, supporting, moving, quickening, and, as in 'Frost at Midnight',
they can be mental rather than physical:

The winds come to me from the fields of sleep.

(*Immortality Ode*)

Winds and mountain rivers and lakes act in concert:

Oh! soul of Nature, excellent and fair,
That didst rejoice with me, with whom I too
Rejoiced, through early youth, before the winds
And powerful waters, and in lights and shades
That march'd and countermarch'd about the hills.

(*Prelude*, Bk. XI, ll. 138–42)

'I was as wakeful', Wordsworth writes, 'Even as waters are
to the sky's motion' (*Prelude*, III, ll. 135–6). Clouds sym-
bolize full integration—the integration which comes from
submission to law and yet is reconciled with 'unfettered'
freedom. The Leech-Gatherer has this quality as he stoops
over the mountain pool:

Upon the margin of that moorish flood
Motionless as a cloud the old Man stood,
That heareth not the loud winds when they call;
And moveth all together if it move at all.

Or Wordsworth will apply the cloud-image to himself, and
give to a simple incident a resonance it would never have
outside the context of his total world:

I wandered lonely as a cloud
That floats on high o'er vales and hills.

The simple lyric is a magical bringing together of all the loaded Wordsworthian items: the dancing flowers, the lake, the breeze, the continuous stars.

Even in a cursory and incomplete list one other group of Wordsworth's main symbolic objects must not be omitted— his imagery of bird, flower, star, and moon. Bird, flower, and star are associated with 'self-joy', happy aloneness. The moon also: but in her case she is submitted to the cycle of change—not a regrettable transience that goes along with decay, but a fulfilling renewal that can come like revelation. The culminating expression of unassailable joy and single-ness is the famous *Intimations* passage:

> The Moon doth with delight
> Look round her when the heavens are bare.

Birds epitomize harmonious and happy activity: for example, the flock of birds in *The Recluse* (where they are also mirrored in the still lake), part of

> the universal imagery
> Inverted, all its sun-bright features touched
> As with the varnish and the gloss of dreams;
> Dreamlike the blending also of the whole
> Harmonious landscape; all along the shore
> The boundary lost, the line invisible
> That parts the image from reality.

(V, p. 332)

Or 'The Green Linnet':

> While birds, and butterflies, and flowers,
> Make all one band of paramours,
> Thou, ranging up and down the bowers,
>   Art sole in thy employment:
> A Life, a Presence like the Air,
> Scattering thy gladness without care,
> Too blest with anyone to pair,
>   Thyself thy own enjoyment.

(II, p. 140)

117

Flowers and stars share the same natural obedience to an ordering that is also a spontaneous *being*. The small celandine remains

> In close self-shelter, like a thing at rest.
>
> (IV, p. 244)

The Daisy (like the daffodils) combines star and flower:

> I see thee glittering from afar—
> And then thou art a pretty star;
> Not quite so fair as many are
> In heaven above thee!
> Yet like a star, with glittering crest,
> Self-poised in air thou seem'st to rest.
>
> (II, p. 139)

With writing of this sort we have maybe passed beyond the poetry of 'wise passiveness'. Ideally, in any case, after the fourth stage—in which the mind opens and adjusts itself to the object—there should be a type of poetry (and experience) in which the transaction is fully reciprocal. Wordsworth had such experiences and they have caused him to be considered a 'mystic'. I imagine 'mysticism' is almost always too prematurely invoked or predicated. At any rate, in personal relations (in successfully falling in love, for example) the inability to distinguish what is given and what is received is universal: 'The Phoenix and the Turtle' is a Shakespearean note on the division and unity that are then revealed as necessary to each other. Wordsworth's 'mysticism' is similar to the kind of experiences Shakespeare tries to define. Only, Wordsworth has the experience not with persons but with things, especially with landscapes wherein river, road, wood, mountain, sky and cloud muster their language for a summatory utterance. The chief instance of this in Wordsworth's work is maybe 'The Simplon Pass'. Here a scene in its totality is fully realized. It is affirmed to be also a whole mind—Wordsworth's, Mind generally, and God:

                    Brook and road
        Were fellow-travellers in this gloomy Pass,
        And with them did we journey several hours
        At a slow step. The immeasurable height
        Of woods decaying, never to be decayed,
        The stationary blasts of waterfalls,
        And in the narrow rent at every turn
        Winds thwarting winds, bewildered and forlorn,
        The torrents shooting from the clear blue sky,
        The rocks that muttered close upon our ears,
        Black drizzling crags that spake by the wayside
        As if a voice were in them, the sick sight
        And giddy prospect of the raving stream,
        The unfettered clouds and region of the heavens,
        Tumult and peace, the darkness and the light—
        Were all like workings of one mind, the features
        Of the same face, blossoms upon one tree,
        Characters of the great Apocalypse,
        The types and symbols of Eternity,
        Of first, and last, and midst, and without end.

                                    (II, pp. 212–13)

The reader unacclimatized to Wordsworth's landscape of the
mind is maybe less likely to accept a passage like this in
isolation than he is 'There was a Boy'. Wordsworth here,
explicitly, makes the largest claims. A Jungian might point
to the indications of a genuine emergence of the transcendent. The scene described is a unity of four spheres: the
'unfettered clouds and a region of the heavens', the 'woods
decaying, never to be decayed', the space of conflict and
frustration where winds thwart winds, and finally (the ultimate issue of 'torrents shooting from the clear blue sky') the
'giddy prospect of the raving stream'. There can be no doubt
of the roominess of the nature revealed and the extremes that
nature embraces: tumult and peace, the darkness and the
light, imprisoning frustration and ordered energy, impetu-
ous direction and chaotically headlong self-turbulence.
The whole passage could stand as an immediate refutation

of Huxley's argument in 'Wordsworth in the Tropics'.

'The Simplon Pass' is unusual for Wordsworth. Not only is there the sudden excessiveness of its claim, there is also a notable lapse from the tranquillity with which Wordsworth usually recollects the past. Infantile or primitive emotion comes in more than a little. *Gloomy* pass is a more crudely 'romantic' note than we normally expect. So too is the projection in

> Black drizzling crags that spake by the wayside
> As if a voice were in them.

(The first line of this Wordsworth is recalling from something he wrote in 1793.) The whole passage is disturbed, as if the various strata of the Wordsworthian universe were faulting. The 'giddy prospect of the raving stream' is placed next to 'the unfettered clouds and region of the heavens'— the polar opposites of the Wordsworth world. The third term, the 'torrents shooting from the clear blue sky', has occurred much earlier. And in an almost dream-like transition we slip from 'workings of one mind', through 'features of the same face, blossoms upon one tree', to

> Characters of the great Apocalypse,
> The types and symbols of Eternity,
> Of first, and last, and midst, and without End.

There is a pervading feeling of seismic disturbance. The phatic 'immeasurable' sits by the subtler, more normally Wordsworthian 'woods decaying never to be decayed'. These might be the deciduous life of the mind and its ceaseless seasonal deaths and renewals (seasonal over centuries, that is: Wordsworth is looking at conifer forests where though the individual dies, nevertheless the forest remains). It is certainly the same perception of the passing and the recurrent in phenomena already noticed in 'There was a Boy'. 'Stationary blasts' has this too: the synaesthesia of sight and sound and concept, the age-long roar that is sensed as a momentary blast. The combination of unusual disturbance and unusual span with the more usual Wordsworth who can assess the weight of his experiences and subtly control his language so as to convey both experience and assessment—this tends to carry 'The Simplon Pass' to us, again, as a piece of truth rather than fiction.

IV

Wordsworth's expectations from Nature are different from those of Coleridge as expressed in 'Frost at Midnight'. It might be remembered, too, that when Wordsworth addressed a poem to the little Hartley he wrote:

> I thought of times when Pain might be thy guest,
> Lord of thy house and hospitality;
> And Grief, uneasy lover! never rest
> But when she sate within the touch of thee.
> O too industrious folly!
> O vain and causeless melancholy!
> Nature will either end thee quite;
> Or, lengthening out thy season of delight,
> Preserve for thee, by individual right,
> A young lamb's heart among the full-grown flocks.

There is no naïve mechanical trust. In a rejected passage from 'The Recluse' (January 1800), written at a time when he was ecstatically looking forward to settling in Grasmere, Wordsworth also wrote:

> in my day of Childhood I was less
> The mind of Nature, less, take all in all,
> Whatever may be lost, than I am now.

> (IV, p. 316)

The period 1798–1802 begins and ends with sombre undertones in Wordsworth's 'nature'-poetry. 'The Simplon Pass' embraces the darkness and the light, but it is itself an unusual moment. What did Wordsworth carry over from his deepest sense of union and severance into the normal situations of his continuing existence? The answer both to this question and to the question proposed by 'Tintern Abbey''s evasive 'still sad music of humanity' is maybe to be found in such poems as 'The Solitary Reaper'—a mature companion-piece and counterpart to 'The Reverie of Poor Susan'.

Wordsworth's central achievement is a curious composedness *in himself*. He was a man, Coleridge said (making a theological joke) for whom it was good that he should be alone. 'The Solitary Reaper' is one of Wordsworth's largest and most complex statements concerning the alone-ness in which he found his balance:

> Behold her, single in the field,
> Yon solitary Highland Lass!
> Reaping and singing by herself;
> Stop here, or gently pass!
> Alone she cuts and binds the grain,
> And sings a melancholy strain;
> O listen! for the Vale profound
> Is overflowing with the sound.
>
> No nightingale did ever chaunt
> More welcome notes to weary bands
> Of travellers in some shady haunt,
> Among Arabian sands:
> A voice so thrilling ne'er was heard
> In Spring-time from the Cuckoo-bird,
> Breaking the silence of the seas
> Among the farthest Hebrides.
>
> Will no-one tell me what she sings?—
> Perhaps the plaintive numbers flow
> For old, unhappy, far-off things,
> And battles long ago:
> Or is it some more humble lay,
> Familiar matter of today?
> Some natural sorrow, loss, or pain,
> That has been and will be again?

Whate'er the theme, the Maiden sang
As if her song could have no ending;
I saw her singing at her work
And o'er the sickle bending;—
I listened, motionless and still,
And, as I mounted up the hill,
The music in my heart I bore,
Long after it was heard no more.

The largeness and complexity of the poem consist in the
kind of solitariness Wordsworth is relating himself to, and
the relation he enjoys with it. The Whitehead word is not
inappropriate: Wordsworth at the end of the poem is curiously *comfortable*. It is significant, for example, that the line

I listened, motionless and still

originally stood as:

I listened till I had my fill.

Originally, as the poet turned away from the girl to continue
his own solitary journey, he was filled with a sense of satisfaction amounting to repletion. The comfortableness is a
strange yet typically Wordsworthian thing to emerge from
the experience we are led through by the poem.

The girl, like Poor Susan, is a working girl. She is alone,
she is working, and she is singing. This girl is, so to speak,
both Poor Susan and the song of the thrush. Presumably she
has never been away from her glen, yet, significantly, there is
no suggestion that she is 'at home' in this countryside. More
significantly still, her song is not a happy one, as, in spite of
the cage, the thrush's might have been. Rather, her song has
all the 'melancholy' the thrush's would have had if, like Poor
Susan, or like Wordsworth himself, the bird had been fully
aware of the cage, its deprivations, and the set conditions
enforcing it. The first verse carries us with a kind of awed
gentleness into the presence of the girl's loneliness, with its
toil, its sadness, and its melody:

> Alone she cuts and binds the grain,
> And sings a melancholy strain.

Then the song is suddenly magnified and made to seem the voice of the whole landscape in which the girl is included. It is almost unified with the natural background:

> O listen! for the Vale profound
> Is overflowing with the sound.

'Profound' and 'overflowing' are unobtrusive displacements of meaning. The Vale reaches down to central depths, physical profundities. It is also profound in that what it says (through the song) is deep and meaningful.

The verse that follows is another favourite quotation from Wordsworth that is very seldom read. A curious feature of it is the welcome Wordsworth seems to accord the song. He is a desert traveller struggling towards the longed-for oasis. The girl is a nightingale in the oasis's 'shady haunt', but it is irrelevant in a Wordsworth context to remember that the nightingale is a sad bird, that it sings with its breast on a thorn, and commemorates a myth in which maidenhood was 'so rudely forc'd'. The nightingale image is followed by the cuckoo. And again there is a suggestion of joy and relief at the bird's song coming as it does in spring-time, after the wintry desert. Yet with magical rapidity the spring-time promise and the cuckoo's sequestered note are swallowed up in

> the silence of the seas
> Among the farthest Hebrides.

The cuckoo is a more successful vehicle for the meanings Wordsworth wants to bring together. The cuckoo in its environing sea is the girl in her total situation. Wordsworth has summoned up the vast, overflowing expressiveness of the melancholy strain and enclosed it in the vaster distances and anti-vital quietudes beyond the Hebrides. He has reduced the song, so to speak, to the scale at which we are reminded vividly again of the girl, her pathetic smallness and isolation.

Her notes are as plaintive, as distant, and as reiteratively limited as the cuckoo's. Instead of becoming a Goddess interpreting the soul of Nature, she remains a girl working and singing in a field.

We are prepared by the last lines of the second verse for the specific attention the third verse then bestows upon the Highland Lass as *this particular girl*—a girl as particularly realized as Poor Susan. Perhaps it is a traditional heroic ballad she is singing, or, alternatively, something like a Burns lyric? For a moment Wordsworth almost sounds as if it were desperately important to know precisely what the song was about. But he quickly recalls himself. The song is what was sung once, is being sung now, and will be sung again. It is the permanent song of all human beings at all times everywhere, and has to be felt and sung afresh by each one in the solitude of his situation. Part of the 'comfortableness' (it is not the right word) of the last verse comes from the recognition of this permanency and inescapability: the recognition, too, that the girl's situation is not singular to her, but is Wordsworth's and everybody's:

> Whate'er the theme, the Maiden sang
> As if her song could have no ending;
> I saw her singing at her work
> And o'er her sickle bending.

Wordsworth avoids all the commonplace sentimentalities the situation of the poem might lend itself to. He neither compassionates, nor envies, nor condescends, nor idealizes. He is not the town-dweller finding simple happiness in the countryside. He is not the literary man with a nostalgia for the 'rootedness' of workers in the fields. (The girl is singularly not 'rooted', not 'a part of', or 'at one with', or 'at home in' Nature.) Neither is he at all inclined to rush to relieve the girl's loneliness or the hardness of her lot. Wordsworth is not concerned to alter in any way the situation he contemplates. His toughness as well as his tenderness are

equivalent to those he responds to in the girl. Nor is he
stoically impassive; and complacent indifference to the girl's
situation is the last thing that could be alleged. Neither comfort nor discomfort are adequate to define the complexity of
what we are left with at the end. Nor is solitude the right
word for what Wordsworth sees as the pathos of the Solitary
Reaper: for the solitude, to repeat, is not a singular thing.
Something metaphysical rather than psychological seems
required to do the perceptions justice. Adapting a sentence
of Coleridge's we might say that the medium whereby spirits
communicate is the solitude and freedom they have in
common, and that this is what Wordsworth's poem is
defining.

Wordsworth, at the end, turns his back on the girl. I think
his revision of the final verse was a mistake. We need the
deep sense of satisfaction that the song has brought with it
—the sense of repletion which sets Wordsworth free to turn
away, on his own axis, and continue in his own vast orbit:

> I listened till I had my fill,
> And, as I mounted up the hill,
> The music in my heart I bore
> Long after it was heard no more.

'I have learned', Wordsworth wrote in 1798,

> To look on nature, not as in the hour
> Of thoughtless youth; but hearing oftentimes
> The still sad music of humanity.

What this last line means can only be understood in terms of
such poems as 'The Solitary Reaper'. Neither man nor
nature are opposed. Nor are they one. Both are related to a
fuller context that includes them, the expression of which is
the song the girl sang. Wordsworth's symbol for the containing situation is commonly not a scene but a monolithic
figure in an empty landscape. And that figure (either
Michael, or the Leech-Gatherer, or the Highland girl) is the
metaphysical 'I'— the 'I' which insulates us and yet is the

very means whereby we have communion with things and with other I's.

'The Solitary Reaper' indicates the kind of link there is between such poems as 'The Reverie of Poor Susan' and 'Tintern Abbey'. These last are complementary. They emanate from the Wordsworthian centre in which both 'nature' and 'humanity' are thought of as one.

V

THE APOTHEOSIS OF
THE ANIMAL

THE Wordsworth that seems to emerge from the poems of
1797–1807 is a poet trying to discover what it is to be a
living mind. He is interested in the child drinking in passion
from its mother's eye and in the old man about whom he can
wonder how is it that he lives. He is interested in the parent
principle of responsiveness, and, equally, in the balancing
activity of consolidation. He is really the poet of middle-age.
The child and the old man abide as problems. 'The Small
Celandine' is a stark statement of the unrelieved paradox, of
the two extremities between which man must run his course:

> I stopped, and said with inly-muttered voice,
> 'It doth not love the shower, nor seek the cold:
> This neither is its courage nor its choice,
> But its necessity in being old.'

The poems on old age (and Wordsworth had his vision of
old age when he was very young) are as central as the poems
on childhood. Wordsworth, as poet and as man, strives to
bring the two into relation. Wordsworth is, above all, the
poet of man's mortality, brooding over the complete organic

cycle. It is only with the poets who come after Wordsworth that an attempt is made to arrest the movement of life at some point in youth or earlier.

In Sussex (as Bradley supposed) or in the Tropics (with Aldous Huxley) this central concern would have been the same. There is, however, truth in Bradley's contention that Cumberland, for all that, occupies a place of importance. Cumberland surrounded Wordsworth with a language of sublimity; it provided him with a norm of what human nature could endure and achieve, in embodied activity. It is difficult at some point in any discussion of Wordsworth to avoid the kind of remark Bradley made in connexion with Wordsworth's evidences of immortality:

> For me, I confess, all this is far from being 'mere poetry'—partly because I do not believe that any such thing as 'mere poetry' exists. But whatever kind or degree of truth we may find in all this, everything in Wordsworth that is sublime or approaches sublimity has, directly or more remotely, to do with it. And without this part of his poetry Wordsworth would be 'shorn of his strength', and would no longer stand, as he does stand, nearer than any other poet of the Nineteenth Century to Milton.
>
> (*Oxford Lectures on Poetry*)

To accept Wordsworth's poetry we must accept his 'active universe' and the possibility of interaction between it and its indwellers. Wordsworth explored a language things had with him and with each other. He forced poetry into a path where, afterwards, it would have to be a real transaction (a kind of truth) or nothing.

However, the central thing in Wordsworth, as we may have even over-insisted, is not 'nature', but the mysterious principle (under the influence of eighteenth-century psychology he called it a principle of pleasure), the mysterious power that makes interchange between man and his universe possible. As we have seen, the arc described by the poetry written during the decade 1797–1807 only incidentally takes in the joy of youth and the deep joy of the nature-communicant.

Lyrical Ballads is devoted mainly to pointing out the dislocation between man and nature. Even while the later books of *The Prelude* were being written, so were 'Resolution and Independence' and the 'Ode on the Intimations', the one asking of decrepit and poverty-stricken childless Age how is it that it *lives*, the other reconciling itself to what life is left in the embers of lived experience. Wordsworth's poetry in the main is elegiac in its feeling. The quick of living is over. What remains is to endure without repining, and without despair.

Put like this it might appear that Wordsworth's main attitudes collapse back on to something simple and negative, some kind of 'stoicism' that he has often been charged with. This is certainly not true, though his position can easily be misconceived or over-simplified. Wordsworth's difficulty was that the epiphany on which he based the optimistic reading of *The Prelude* was unrepeatable, and this 'mystical' element he gave a prime value to. Life thereafter could only offer, apparently, memories and resignation. The startling thing is that after *The Prelude* Wordsworth wrote 'The White Doe of Rylstone'. And in this poem he opened out new territory, psychological as well as literary. In many ways 'The White Doe' is Wordsworth's strangest, and in some ways his profoundest, exercise of the spirit. Wordsworth himself suggests the large scale to which it should be referred. It is, after Milton, a new statement of 'the fortitude of patience and heroic martyrdom' (III, p. 543). As a major re-orientation of the Wordsworthian universe we propose to treat it.

The Dedication (an address to his wife) tells how the poem brought (to them both) a consolation as deep as that they had found in Spenser's story of Una:

> Then, too, this Song of *mine* once more would please,
> Where anguish, strange as dreams of restless sleep,
> Is tempered and allayed by sympathies
> Aloft ascending and descending deep,

Even to the inferior kinds; whom forest-trees
Protect from beating sun-beams, and the sweep
Of the sharp winds;—fair Creatures!—to whom Heaven
A calm and sinless life, with love, has given.

This tragic Story cheered us; for it speaks
Of female patience winning firm repose;
And, of the recompense that conscience seeks,
A bright, encouraging example shows;
Needful when o'er wide realms the tempest breaks,
Needful amid life's ordinary woes;—
Hence, not for them unfitted who would bless
A happy hour with holier happiness.

'The White Doe' reverts to something like the narrative poem Wordsworth experimented with in *Lyrical Ballads*. Yet it steps outside the closed eighteenth-century psychology which limits the applicability of 'Peter Bell' (of the same period as *Lyrical Ballads*). Superficially it reminds one of 'Christabel' or 'Marmion'. But it is more than romantic mediaevalism. Wordsworth specifically avoids archaism, or the triviality of writing in a *genre*. The poem has its own psychological and moral interest. It is a new venture of the Wordsworthian mind. Yet it is detached from what up to 1807 Wordsworth had made Wordsworthianism seem. It amounts to a new distribution of the Wordsworthian insights and emphases.

This is a lot to claim for one of the least typical of Wordsworth's poems. Yet it may be recalled Wordsworth made some such claim himself: 'he considered "The White Doe" as, in conception, the highest work he had ever produced'. (III, p. 548.) Or, again: '"The White Doe" starts from a high point of imagination, and comes round, through various wanderings of that faculty, to a still higher—nothing less than the Apotheosis of the Animal. . . . And as this poem thus begins and ends with lofty Imagination, every motive and impetus that actuates the persons introduced is from the same source; a kindred spirit pervades, and is intended to harmonize, the whole.'

Wordsworth's epigraph for the poem includes a quotation from his early play *The Borderers* (written in 1796):

> Action is transitory—a step, a blow,
> The motion of a muscle—this way or that—
> 'Tis done; and in the after vacancy
> We wonder at ourselves like men betrayed;
> Suffering is permanent, obscure and dark,
> And has the nature of infinity.

This curiously by-passes the experience of *The Prelude*. It seems almost an inversion of the 'joy' in communion with things (and with infinity) Wordsworth there asserts to be primary. The spiritual crux of 'The White Doe' concerns the positives that are in suffering.

Wordsworth took his material from Percy's *Reliques*, and from local traditions connected with the Rising of the Northern Earls. Norton, the father of nine sons and a daughter, rebels on behalf of the old religion. Though the motives of the leaders of the revolt are ambiguous, his are sincere. Wordsworth treats him, and, because of him, his cause, with considerable sympathy. The old man's devotion to St. Cuthbert, and to the banner of the Cross and the Five Wounds, is throughout respected. One of the outstanding features of 'The White Doe', however (one we might expect from Wordsworth now) is the detachment as well as the sympathy he brings to a topic that could easily lend itself to a stock handling. The banner is embroidered with the Cross and the Five Wounds, certainly. But it is also being used in a civil war. Unconsciously Norton has reduced it to the level of a personal totem. Wordsworth is aware of the ambiguous motive behind the whole Rising. Softly accented as the irony is it is inescapable:

> Two earls fast leagued in discontent
> Who gave their wishes open vent;

And boldly urged a general plea,
The rites of ancient piety
To be triumphantly restored
By the stern justice of the sword.

The religious motive masks a private discontent. Wordsworth notes the contradiction between the means and the end, between ancient piety and the civil war needed to re-establish it. A similar note is taken of the Banner. What it really symbolizes is desecrated by the use it is being put to:

And that same Banner in whose breast
The blameless Lady had exprest
Memorials chosen to give life
And sunshine to a dangerous strife;
That Banner, waiting for the Call,
Stood quietly in Rylstone Hall.

The force is in the 'quietly' of the last line. What the Banner is in itself, as well as what it is for Emily, is altogether different from what the father would make of it.

The Rebellion is a sixteenth-century analogue of the early 1790's. All the terms are transposed but the basic structure is preserved of a situation which divides (every way) society, the family, and the individual—which insists either on action or passive withdrawal and yet cannot be completely satisfied with either. For the believer in Humanity the outbreak of the wars with France was experienced as a kind of Civil War. And if he were sufficiently conscious the individual had to choose his side. Wordsworth's experience of the 1790's possibly accounts for his range of sympathy in 'The White Doe'. The groups involved in the Rising are various. The father is single-minded, devout, and passionate. His sons are even more simple. Their loyalty is the expression of an automatic family-solidarity:

Gone are they, bravely, though misled,
With a dear Father at their head!
The Sons obey a natural lord.

133

Again Wordsworth's accent on '*natural* lord' is quiet but telling. The family, however, is not united. Francis and Emily have been brought up by their now dead mother as adherents to the Reformed Church. Francis's is the consciousness which knows the two sides of the division most deeply. He is aware of the untimeliness and immaturity of the Rebellion, of the imperfect motive in its supporters, of its inherent unlikelihood of success. He disbelieves in the aim and disapproves of the means: the awareness isolates and paralyses him. Yet he loves his father and brothers and must go with them, though he cannot suppress his knowledge of all the rest he owes allegiance to. Wordsworth handles Francis's predicament with fine perceptiveness:

> Thus, with his sons, where forth he came
> The sight was hailed with loud acclaim
> And din of arms and minstrelsy,
> From all his warlike tennantry,
> All horsed and harnessed with him to ride,—
> A voice to which the hills replied!
>
> But Francis, in the vacant hall,
> Stood silent under dreary weight,—
> A phantasm, in which roof and wall
> Shook, tottered, swam before his sight;
> A phantasm like a dream of night!
> Thus overwhelmed, and desolate,
> He found his way to a postern gate;
> And when he waked, his languid eye
> Was on the calm and silent sky;
> With air about him breathing sweet,
> And earth's green grass beneath his feet;
> Nor did he fail e'er long to hear
> A sound of military cheer,
> Faint—but it reached that sheltered spot;
> He heard, and it disturbed him not.
>
> There stood he, leaning on a lance
> Which he had grasped unknowingly,

Had blindly grasped in that strong trance,
That dimness of heart-agony;
There stood he, cleansed from the despair
And sorrow of his fruitless prayer.
The past he calmly hath reviewed:
But where will be the fortitude
Of this brave man, when he shall see
That Form beneath the spreading tree
And know that it is Emily?

Francis's situation is similar to that of the young English Republican in the 1790's. Then too neither flight nor fight was an adequate solution. In the 1790's Wordsworth had come to see action as either transitory or impossible. After the period of vacancy with its sense of betrayal had come *Lyrical Ballads* and the beginnings of *The Prelude*. From thoughts of humanity-in-general, to be saved by the intervention of embattled groups, Wordsworth had emancipated himself. He turned to the infinities which open out before and within the particular person. So Francis is aware of a conflict that is also a deadlock: hence his black-out. When he comes round it is notable that his eye rests on a landscape integrated and quiet, like that of 'The Idiot Boy', a landscape healthful, spacious, and everywhere. (Wordsworth's use of the natural symbolism, here again, is disciplined and unobtrusive.) Francis sees the quiet and wholeness of the 'Tintern Abbey' landscape, but none of the 'Tintern Abbey' consolations are admitted. Nor are we left with the stock situation of the hero tragically destroyed between two incompatible loyalties. Francis (and the Wordsworthian movement of imagination) proceeds to envisage a suffering that will not be futilely negative. It is the sister of Francis who has to bear the burden of the new adjustment. Emily carries Wordsworth's meaning for what suffering holds of 'permanent, obscure, and dark' but which also partakes of infinity. Suffering in itself, in the poem, is not a value. Nor are frustration and defeat in however good a cause. Suffering may be inevitable but it is also accidental.

135

The real values are in what you suffer for, or in what you find through suffering. Emily must assert these values. They are above and beyond the conflict—above its blind heroisms and wilful sacrifices, beyond its base betrayals and wrongful recriminations. What happens in Emily afterwards will be something she owes both to the victors and the vanquished. (There is an odd kinship, in more places than one, between Wordsworth's thought in 'The White Doe' and Eliot's in 'The Four Quartets'.) This, at first, Emily cannot understand. Francis has to present the situation to her. His speech is an amazing example of psychic weaning, of the care that does not care:

> For thee, for thee is left the sense
> Of trial past without offence
> To God or Man; such innocence,
> Such consolation, and the excess
> Of an unmerited distress;
> In that thy very strength must lie.
> —O Sister, I could prophesy!
> The time is come that rings the knell
> Of all we loved, and loved so well:
> Hope nothing, if I thus may speak
> To thee, a woman, and thence weak:
> Hope nothing, I repeat; for we
> Are doomed to perish utterly:
> 'Tis meet that thou with me divide
> The thought while I am by thy side,
> Acknowledging a grace in this,
> A comfort in the dark abyss.
> But look not for me when I am gone,
> And be no farther wrought upon:
> Farewell all wishes, all debate,
> All prayers for this cause or for that!
> Weep, if that aid thee; but depend
> Upon no help of outward friend;
> Espouse thy doom at once, and cleave
> To fortitude without reprieve.

Emily's position is only definable in terms of negatives. It is not partisanship of one side or the other. It is not indifference to both. It is not the waste Francis dedicates himself to in a charity of self-squandering magnanimity, the romantic situation of noble defeat in a misconceived and self-doomed cause. Neither is it the helplessness of frustration or the ineffectuality of irrelevance. Wordsworth can hardly be expected to do more than suggest the spiritual secret that is shared between Emily and the White Doe. Emily is to realize a fulfilment that Francis can guess lies beyond his own twilight position. One of Wordsworth's fine touches in his handling of the situation here is that Emily herself cannot see what it is she must become. But her temptation will be, as Francis foresaw, to hope for the wrong things—for the safety of her family, the gifts of fortune or war.

While the final outcome of the Rising is still in doubt a messenger arrives from York. We then see Emily poised between 'hope . . . a rejected stay' and

> that most lamentable snare,
> The self-reliance of despair.

The messenger tries to foster the irrelevant hope. Emily's response harmonizes with the now fully-realized import of Francis's parting words to her:

> 'Ah tempt me not!' she faintly sighed;
> 'I will not counsel nor exhort,—
> With my condition satisfied.'

It would have been useless, in any case, to hope for the return of her father and brothers:

> But quick the turns of chance and change,
> And knowledge has a narrow range;
> Whence idle fears, and needless pain,
> And wishes blind, and efforts vain.—
> The Moon may shine, but cannot be
> Their guide in flight—already she
> Hath witnessed their captivity.

> She saw the desperate assault
> Upon that hostile castle made;—
> But dark and dismal is the vault
> Where Norton and his sons are laid!

Wordsworth continues to use the natural imagery as a backdrop for the story. It is ambivalent imagery, suggesting indisruptible harmonies below and beyond the human: indicating what human nature is cast out from and what it must make its goal to return to. The Moon in this passage, for example—it neither promises safety nor sympathizes with defeat. The universe of the poem is an exacting one. It offers no easy consolations, yet it is not ironically unconcerned. The Moon presides also over the final disaster:

> But ere the Moon had sunk to rest
> In her pale chambers of the west
> Of that rash levy nought remained.

In prison awaiting execution, the father commends the banner to Francis's charge. He has now learned the wisdom of Francis's original counsel, and the wisdom of the perdurable qualities incarnate in Emily and the Doe. The natural imagery is thrown now against the imagery of the ruined shrine. It is as if Norton perceived the supersession by a wider piety of all that he had fought for:

> Bear it to Bolton Priory,
> And lay it on St. Mary's shrine;
> To wither in the sun and breeze
> 'Mid those decaying sanctities.

'Wither' in its context has a rich force. When the Norton family is called to execution, again the same imagery is invoked:

> They rose—embraces none were given—
> They stood like trees when earth and heaven
> Are calm; they knew each other's worth.

This is the apotheosising Wordsworthian vision. Admiration

is never withdrawn from Norton, unrealizable as the end was at which he aimed, and misguided as he was in his stand. Nor is the family solidarity of the loyal sons impugned. Within their limits (and Wordsworth's whole poem exists to reveal the limits) both the father and the sons are heroic.

The family executed, and Francis slain, Emily is left with the burden of remaining alive, allowed no easy hope and forbidden to despair. She is complete in her desolation but also in her regality and patience:

> 'Tis done;—despoil and desolation
> O'er Rylstone's fair domain have blown;
> Pools, terraces, and walks are sown
> With weeds; the bowers are overthrown,
> Or have given way to slow mutation,
> While, in their ancient habitation
> The Norton name hath been unknown.
> The lordly mansion of its pride
> Is stripped; the ravage hath spread wide
> Through park and field, a perishing
> That mocks the gladness of the Spring!
> And, with this silent gloom agreeing,
> Appears a joyless human Being,
> Of aspect such as if the waste
> Were under her dominion placed.
> Upon a primrose bank, her throne
> Of quietness, she sits alone;
> Among the ruins of a wood,
> Erewhile a covert bright and green,
> And where full many a brave tree stood,
> That used to spread its boughs, and ring
> With the sweet birds' carolling.
> Behold her, like a Virgin Queen,
> Neglecting in imperial state
> These outward images of fate,
> And carrying inward a serene
> And perfect sway, through many a thought
> Of chance and change, that hath been brought
> To the subjection of a holy,

> Though stern and rigorous, melancholy!
> The like authority, with grace
> Of awfulness, is in her face,—
> There hath she fixed it; yet it seems
> To o'ershadow by no native right
> That face which cannot lose the gleams,
> Lose utterly the tender gleams,
> Of gentleness and meek delight,
> And loving-kindness ever bright:
> Such is her sovereign mien:—her dress
> (A vest with woollen cincture tied,
> A hood of mountain-wool undyed)
> Is homely,—fashioned to express
> A wandering Pilgrim's humbleness.

Patience that could guarantee its reward would be no patience. Emily has nothing of the complacency of long-term self-righteousness. Wordsworth resorts again to natural imagery to define her state—oak-like (and lucky) endurance, sequestration, fragility, vulnerability, the uniqueness of the girl's flower-like persistence in sorrow, and the contrast with 'the gladsome earth':

> And so,—beneath a mouldered tree,
> A self-surviving leafless oak
> By unregarded age from stroke
> Of ravage saved—sate Emily.
> There did she rest, with head reclined,
> Herself most like a stately flower,
> (Such have I seen) whom chance of birth
> Hath separated from its kind,
> To live and die in a shady bower,
> Single on the gladsome earth.

Emily, finally, is visited by the White Doe, which attaches itself to her. With the White Doe Emily re-establishes herself in a world where she has lost her family but now can find her home. Wordsworth is careful not to exaggerate what Emily stands for, or in fact achieves. There is no attempt to make her either saint or tragedy-queen. With his unremitting

sense of the preciousness of normality and the importance of
common human quality he leaves her at the end of the poem
merely deepened and strengthened by the wave of adversity
that has passed over her:

> But most to Bolton's sacred Pile,
> On favouring nights, she loved to go;
> There ranged through cloister, court and aisle,
> Attended by the soft-paced Doe;
> Nor feared she in the still moonshine
> To look upon Saint Mary's shrine;
> Nor on the lonely turf that showed
> Where Francis slept in his last abode.
> For that she came, there oft she sate
> Forlorn, but not disconsolate:
> And, when she from the abyss returned
> Of thought, she neither shrunk nor mourned;
> Was happy that she lived to greet
> Her mute companion as it lay
> In love and pity at her feet;
> How happy in its turn to meet
> The recognition! the mild glance
> Beamed from that gracious countenance;
> Communication like the ray
> Of a new morning, to the nature
> And prospects of the inferior Creature!

Wordsworth considered 'the Apotheosis of the Ánimal'
to be his finest imaginative conception. Nor is it merely conception. The Doe is a highly successful poetic presence. As
the poem unwinds the creature is revealed as ministrant,
monitor, and avatar—all three together and only any one
separately because it is also the others. The Doe is not merely
natural like the Owls the Boy called to, nor supernatural like
the Donkey Peter Bell came upon, nor a 'symbol of self-joy'
like the Green Linnet. With the Doe Wordsworth realizes a
new co-adunation of his major meanings. Human, natural,
and divine, are brought into a final relationship.

We have already suggested that the poem as a whole

indicates a redistribution of the Wordsworthian emphases. This re-ordering is especially clear in the case of the Doe. As animal, it is kept strictly subordinate to the human. (There is no direction to man, now, to go and live with animals, or be the Green Linnet.) But the Doe also participates in the indisruptible Nature that unites law and impulse. Wordsworth no longer gives these qualities to any conceivable—even if dead—Lucy. Yet even as a creature the Doe points to a super-harmony also into which the human must ultimately incorporate itself. Being is unitary. The contraries of saint-like beatification and animal innocence are not in conflict. Average living is held taut between the two.

Wordsworth's thought is surprisingly traditional. Man is between the animal and the angel. The natural sphere cannot know division. The supernatural cannot know less than joy. Between the two is Emily and 'the fortitude of patience'. Wordsworth's Doe is a subtler creation than Lawrence's stallion. In the animal and the girl together Wordsworth was striving to define a natural catholicity, a catholicity deeper than what the Priory could express, yet also one which the ruined shrine would approve even if the congregation meeting there each Sunday could not understand it. The Doe stepping through the dilapidated masonry restores new life and meaning to a ravaged tradition. Similarly, though nature re-invades the nave it also clings to it, finds support in it, and connects it with a more than institutional reality. Beginning where his poem should end, as Words worth says, he describes the Doe visiting Emily's tomb:

> The only voice which you can hear
> Is the river murmuring near.
> —When soft!—the dusky trees between,
> And down the path from the open green,
> Where is no living thing to be seen;
> And through yon gateway, where is found,
> Beneath the arch with ivy bound,
> Free entrance to the church-yard ground—

Comes gliding in with lovely gleam,
Comes gliding in serene and slow,
Soft and silent as a dream,
A solitary Doe!
White she is as lily of June,
And beauteous as the silver moon
When out of sight the clouds are driven
And she is left alone in heaven;
Or like a ship some gentle day
In sunshine sailing far away,
A glittering ship that hath the plain
Of ocean for her own domain.

Lie silent in your graves ye dead!
Lie quiet in your church-yard bed!
Ye living, tend your holy cares;
Ye multitude pursue your prayers;
And blame not me if my heart and sight
Are occupied with one delight!
'Tis a work for sabbath hours
If I with this bright Creature go:
Whether she be of forest bowers,
From the bowers of earth below;
Or a Spirit for one day given,
A pledge of grace from purest heaven.

What harmonious pensive changes
Wait upon her as she ranges
Round and through this Pile of state
Overthrown and desolate!
Now a step or two her way
Leads through space of open day,
Where the enamoured sunny light
Brightens her that was so bright;
Now doth a delicate shadow fall,
Falls upon her like a breath,
From some lofty arch or wall,
As she passes underneath:
Now some gloomy nook partakes

Of the glory that she makes,—
High-ribbed vault of stone, or cell,
With perfect cunning framed as well
Of stone, and ivy, and the spread
Of the elder's bushy head;
Some jealous and forbidden cell,
That doth the living stars repel,
And where no flower hath leave to dwell.

The presence of this wandering Doe
Fills many a damp obscure recess
With lustre of a saintly show;
And, re-appearing, she no less
Sheds on the flowers that round her blow
A more than sunny liveliness.

Ending the poem where it begins, Wordsworth tells how the Doe

walks amid the mournful waste
Of prostrate altars, shrines defaced,
And floors encumbered with rich show
Of fret-work imagery laid low;
Paces softly, or makes halt,
By fractured cell, or tomb, or vault;
By plate of monumental brass
Dim-gleaming among weeds and grass
And sculptured Forms of Warriors brave:
But chiefly by that single grave,
That one sequestered hillock green,
The pensive visitant is seen.
There doth the gentle creature lie
With those adversities unmoved;
Calm spectacle, by earth and sky
In their benignity approved!
And aye, methinks, the hoary Pile,
Subdued by outrage and decay,
Looks down upon her with a smile,
A gracious smile that seems to say—
'Thou, thou art not a Child of Time,
But daughter of the Eternal Prime.'

Wordsworth in 'The White Doe' is not a Wordsworthian. He sees Nature involved in a unity that is more than organic. This order also includes 'the still, sad music of humanity'. The still sad music indeed is its most intimate voice. In the final harmony the sadness and the music have to be reckoned together.

EPILOGUE

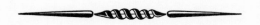

W ORDSWORTH, we have said, was the last great representative in English Poetry of the renaissance tradition. Though he is a mutation within the tradition he is still in the same line as Chaucer, Spenser, Sidney, and Milton. This tradition was imbued with the idea of public service. (Each of those mentioned was in fact a kind of civil servant.) Poets, either by birth, education, loyalty, or election, or all four together, were members of the governing élite. They were the voices of those sanities and wisdoms they conceived as necessary for the public welfare. They wrote from their capacities, they addressed themselves to the active capacities of their audience. An implicit moral purpose (profit countenancing delight) circumscribed what they wrote. Adopting a convenient metaphor, the tradition might be called masculine in its aims and performance.

Wordsworth clearly belongs to this tradition. His strictures on the contemporary reading-public are as notorious as the 'evident design' his poetry had on the moral constitution and the literary taste of his time. His acceptance of government patronage, as well as his Laureateship, was not a defection. It was indeed naturally consonant with what Wordsworth felt profoundly about the poet's place and function. His sonnet-sequences during the Napoleonic wars, his *Convention of Cintra* pamphlet, his persistency of attention to political and social questions—these are the complement of his most personal poetic statements. 'Royalist and conservative as he appeared', Swinburne noted, 'he never really ceased, while his power of song was unimpaired, to be in the deepest and most literal sense a republican.' Discounting all Swinburne's tendentiousness here, Swinburne was in the deepest and most literal sense right. Wordsworth is in the line from Sidney and Milton. 'The White Doe' frankly reverts to traditional values, and to the order of the values instructed traditional wisdom had resolved upon. Not that it is merely a harking-back. Wordsworth in writing it is both developing the tradition and himself advancing, discovering something wider and commoner and more significant than what after him will be called Wordsworthianism. It is in this sense that we have argued Wordsworth is not the poet of Nature so much as the poet of fortitude. Wordsworth was the first of his admirers to relinquish 'Wordsworthianism'.

Wordsworth can be most conveniently 'placed', perhaps, by comparing him with his near-contemporaries, Blake and Keats. And the comparison need not be to Wordsworth's disadvantage.

Wordsworth's fundamental moral attitudes are extremely orthodox. Blake's constitute a real break with orthodoxy. 'Damn braces, bless relaxes', Blake proclaimed, and, 'Everything that lives is holy'. The beginning of wisdom for Blake was the snapping of that tension that exists so long as Reason restrains Desire, establishing a false overlordship, a hierarchy based on suppression and frustration. Imposed law Blake sensed as the root of all evil. Rejecting this false model of sanity-based-on-repression involved him at first in maintaining that 'Everything that lives is holy'. Blake can understand anarchic release or open conflict, he can make poetry from the harsh dichotomies of a divided humanity; what he cannot understand is tension, the mutually enforced compromises that fall short of war and fall short of satisfaction.

For a time (in the period of the earlier Prophetic Books)

Blake's view involved him in an over-excited kind of moral propaganda ('The Vision of the Daughters of Albion', for example) which, in the light of the real as well as the desirable sympathies of mankind, must seem half-baked and repellant.

Eventually the implications of his original insight became more clear. If everything that lives is holy, everything that lives is also unholy—a groaning and a travail of creation for a new creation. The four giants of the mind have equal claims, but their quarrel must issue into 'mutual forgiveness of each vice' before the gates of paradise will be unlocked. Blake's shadowless, a-historic, a-moral present is in immediate juxtaposition to eternity. His is an inorganic and non-human world, profound as his vision is into the contradiction which being human entails.

Keats is at an opposite extreme from Blake, and also (because it is naïve to think that extremes must be limited to two) at an opposite extreme from Wordsworth. Keats was cockney and effeminate, the son of an ostler who went neither to Harrow (as his guardian once envisaged) nor yet to Cambridge: who was therefore outside the main cultural stream, educated to be a leech or a saw-bones rather than a literary man or a governor, initiated into what he called 'the sweets of Poesie' (purple patches from amateur anthologies?) rather than instructed in Homer, Sophocles, Vergil, Horace: —such at least is how he would appear to reviewers writing in the still strong masculine renaissance tradition. There is a wide social and cultural gap between Wordsworth and Keats, wider than the arithmetic of their respective ages would suggest. There is a great shift of centre, too, in poetry. Keats is outside the renaissance tradition completely, and poetry afterwards will follow in his path rather than Wordsworth's. For the barrier between Wordsworth and his predecessors is less high than that which cuts him off from those who succeed him.

Keats objected as strongly to Wordsworth as did Blake.

Consciously at one level, and unconsciously at a much deeper level, Keats was rejecting the whole tradition in which Wordsworth stood. The Renaissance had insisted on combining moral profit with delight. For Keats, poetry that has an open design on us is no-poetry; poetry should simply tell the most heart-easing things. The renaissance poet wrote from his capacities and addressed the capacities of his audience: Keats will write from his incapacities and inadequacies: 'My heart aches, and a drowsy numbness pains my sense'. When this mood was on Wordsworth he waited until it was dissipated by his meeting with the Leech-gatherer before he celebrated it, or celebrated, rather, its correction. Renaissance poetry emanated from the masculine consciousness. Its values are those of order, control, discipline, decision, the wakeful mind that must weigh alternatives and decide between them. Keats was, as they said, effeminate. He relates poetry with sleep. His values are relaxations, receptivenesses, indulgences: in sum, what he called 'indolence', 'negative capability'.

The significance of the Sleep-Poetry equivalence that Keats makes is far-reaching. It inaugurates a poetry dedicated to the expression of the self, but the self as a stream of consciousness, and consciousness as a receptive rather than a deliberative function: the autobiography of chance rather than choice. 'Endymion' is Keats's longest—maybe his biggest—poem in this mode. (The shock of what renaissance-minded reviewers said about it deflected Keats even more than the reception of *Lyrical Ballads* affected Wordsworth.) Here is a characteristic passage in the new and profoundly revolutionary Keatsian mode:

> For many days
> Had he been wandering in uncertain ways:
> Through wilderness, and woods of mossed oaks,
> Counting his woe-worn minutes to the strokes
> Of the lone wood-cutter; and listening still,
> Hour after hour, to each lush-leaved rill.

Now he is sitting by a shady spring,
And elbow-deep with feverous fingering
Stems the upbursting cold: a wild-rose tree
Pavilions him in bloom, and he doth see
A bud which snares his fancy: lo! but now
He plucks it, dips its stalk in water: how
It swells, it buds, it flowers beneath his sight;
And, in the middle, there is softly pight
A golden butterfly; upon whose wings
There must be surely character'd strange things,
For with wide eye he wonders and smiles oft.
  Lightly the little herald flew aloft,
Follow'd by glad Endymion's clasped hands:
Onward it flies. From languor's sullen bands
His limbs are loosed, and eager on he hies,
Dazzled to trace it in the sunny skies.
It seemed he flew, the way so easy was,
And like a new-born spirit did he pass
Through the green evening quiet in the sun.
    (*Endymion*, Bk. II, ll. 47–71)

Any adolescent boy could follow on from here. In the fantasy sleep and poetry co-operate. The transition from image to image is dream-like: the wood of adolescent growth and bewilderment, the wood-cutter who inexorably counts and reduces the items of loneliness that are a constantly diminishing refuge and a constantly growing threat, the living pool that can be deathly except that the rose is there to distract from distraction and open out a new way, the flower of fulfilment, the butterfly-psyche, the chase (contrasting with the inertia of the opening) and the boy loosed to follow gladly 'like a new-born spirit': obviously the poetry cannot be *read*. Each of the items has to do with a process in the mind.

Keats discovered a further significance in the Sleep-Poetry relation. Not only is there the relaxation, indolence, and self-surrender to pleasure which the conjunction of the two suggests; there is also the psychic work that poetry-as-dream can perform. 'Endymion' is a prolonged dream (not

in any literary sense a 'myth') in which a fantasy-solution is
discovered to a permanent adolescent problem: the problem
of the goddess you love and the human girl you must nevertheless marry. Keats's discovery will end, in one direction,
with the psychoanalyst's couch, and, in another, with poetry
as a kind of therapy. Keats himself had an interesting psyche,
with significant tensions to resolve. This gives his poetry
permanent relevance. Lesser people following in his foot-
steps will have maybe lesser and less significant predica-
ments.

Again, Keats made the practice of poetry (as a therapy) an
end in itself. Only in the fantasy and in the act of composing
can the releases and resolutions be found. The work of art is
self-contained, like a dream. It might also be a cul-de-sac.
The lesson of the 'Ode to a Grecian Urn' is that art arrests
the movement of life at the point where life seems to have
reached its maximum, but the arrest is itself a defeat of
fulfilment:

> Bold Lover, never canst thou kiss,
> Though winning near the goal—yet, do not grieve;
> She cannot fade though thou hast not thy bliss,
> For ever wilt thou love, and she be fair!

With Keats, as Dr. Leavis has emphasized, we have the
beginning of a tradition which will dwindle into aestheticism,
when less interesting psyches attempt to monopolize attention and make art the resolution of not widely interesting personal difficulties.

Neither Blake, Keats, nor Wordsworth need suffer from
comparison with each other. It is lucky that English Romanticism produced three such—or, with Coleridge and Byron
added, five such—important individuations. Neither Blake
nor Keats, however, at the moment, need defending. Wordsworth does. The Wordsworth that has been accepted, and
thereafter rejected, is a ghost: a Wordsworth praised or con-
demned for his bucolicism, stoicism, naïve naturism, and

lack of interest in sex. The charges against Wordsworth reflect the inadequacies of the reading public he has had to contend with ever since 1798, equally when his reputation was at its zenith as when it had reached its nadir. He is best seen as at least worthy of respect for the definitions he makes which neither Keats nor Blake could make. Wordsworth is necessary in order to complete the triangle all three are needed to describe. Blake is the poet of religious paradox, of conflict, and of the forgiving heaven of mutuality. Keats is the poet of the human organic: his strategy one of indolence —a relaxation different from that of Blake, for Blake's throwing off of braces leads to a dynamic work of the contraries upon each other, an agony and a struggle. Wordsworth is the poet of a human nature that is not merely organic. Unlike Keats, his emphasis falls on choice and deliberation. Like Blake, Wordsworth knows the conflict in which human nature is involved. Unlike Blake, he is however the poet of moral strenuousness and tension, of the fortitude of patience. It is here that Wordsworth sees the prime values for continuing existence and growth. All three, in their own way, 'damn braces', reject the artificial supports of an eighteenth-century intellectually and morally inadequate. Wordsworth's 'wise passiveness' is as profound as Blake's 'relaxes' or Keats's 'indolence'. Wordsworth is dynamic where Keats is not. Modestly, he is aware of limits and human responsibilities where Blake would reject both. There is no one greater than him, in poetry, since Milton, Coleridge said. It is still difficult to think of a greater poet since, of a poet as aware as Wordsworth was of what the long haul of being human implies.